HONORÉE CORDER
B. HALE

Write

LIKE A

BOSS

FROM A WHISPER
TO A ROAR

The Chronicles of Lumineia

—The Age of Oracles—

The Rogue Mage

The Lost Mage

The Battle Mage

—The Master Thief—

Jack of Thieves

Thief in the Myst

The God Thief

—The Second Draeken War—

Elseerian

The Gathering

Seven Days

The List Unseen

—The Warsworn—

The Flesh of War

The Age of War

The Heart of War

—The White Mage Saga—

Assassin's Blade (Short story prequel)

The Last Oracle

The Sword of Elseerian

Descent Unto Dark

Impact of the Fallen

The Forge of Light

WRITE
LIKE
A BOSS

FROM A WHISPER TO A ROAR!

Paperback ISBN: 978-0-9994780-0-4
Digital ISBN: 978-0-9994780-1-1

Interior Design: Christina Gorchos, 3CsBooks.com

Honorée Corder

B. Hale

GRATITUDE

From Honorée ...

Without the undying support of my husband, I wouldn't be a writer today. Thank you for speaking words of possibility into me every day!

Ben, what a true blessing you are! I cherish our friendship, and our work together is so darn fun it can hardly be called work! Thank you for inspiring me to up my writing game and to write like a boss every day!

To my team: Christina, Dino, and Kevin—ya'll make me look so good! Thank you for your quick and amazing work, I'm blessed to work beside you.

From Ben ...

The list of those who have helped me is as long as my arm, but there are certainly those who've made an enormous difference in my career.

To Honorée, a flawless example of true friendship.

To Kathryn, my editor and ally.

And to my wife, who is perfect.

SPECIAL INVITATION

Many like-minded individuals have gathered in an online community to share ideas, render support, and promote accountability. When I first wrote *Prosperity for Writers*, I envisioned helping numerous writers shatter the belief that they must starve to survive. I had no idea what was in store, and the result is an amazing community of 1300+ writers, authors, editors, and more!

I'd like to personally invite you to join the The Prosperous Writer Mastermind at HonoreeCorder.com/Writers and Facebook.com/groups/ProsperityforWriters where you will find motivation, daily support, and help with any writing or self-publishing questions.

You can connect with me personally on Twitter @Honoree, or on Facebook.com/Honoree. Thank you so much for your most precious resource, your time. I look forward to connecting and hearing about your book soon!

TABLE OF CONTENTS

A NOTE FROM BEN

F ew know this, but I never thought I would be a writer. My English classes in school were a chore and I abhorred grammar. (Doesn't everyone?) Despite my revulsion for writing I loved to read, and at one point I began thinking of my own story. Fifteen years later I mentioned it to my wife and she encouraged me to write the story. I laughed. Seriously, I doubted I had the ability to write. But she kept encouraging me and eventually I gave in. That was nine years ago, and I've now written seventeen books and sold hundreds of thousands of copies. It's become my career, and more importantly, my passion.

The reason I share my story is because if I—who had no desire or talent to speak of—can write, you most certainly can. I've wanted to write this book for a while now but something never seemed to click. The missing piece (and a true friend) came into my life in 2016. Honorée and I both LOVE to encourage aspiring writers and we began toying with the idea of working together. She is the consummate professional yet real at the same time. If you want to be successful, read her books. If you want to find a true supporter, get to know her.

As you read this book I implore you to look critically at your writing process. To write like a boss you must *be* the boss. Writing requires courage, so gather your courage and let's get to work.

Note: when you see this font, it's me, Ben.

A Note from Honorée

I t is with great pleasure I wrote this first book in the *Like a Boss* series with Ben Hale, a first-class gentleman. We met at the *Smarter Artist Summit* in 2016. Even as a mega-successful writer, he is so kind and humble. And man, does he *write like a boss!* Impressed with him, I jumped at the chance to work on a project when he suggested it. Someone said (and to this day, we don't know who) *Write Like a Boss!* And voilà, the first in our series was born! I know you'll find the knowledge he shares to be invaluable.

This book, the first in the series, is designed to help you transform your writing business by giving you the exact information you need to master your writing business and achieve your goals.

I've self-published more than two-dozen books since 2004, and sold over 800,000 copies. In this book and in this series, I'll be sharing what I wish I'd known on day one. I would have been so grateful to have a reference guide to help me abolish negative self-talk, eliminate useless beliefs, know how to be creative when I sat down to write, and be inspired to write more often. This information, combined with other valuable knowledge, would have come in handy. I hope it does for you!

No one is more surprised than I am that I'm a successful, full-time writer. If you come from less-than-ideal beginnings, as I do, then take this note as a sign you can live the dream. I promise you can!

Note: this is my font!

Let's do this, shall we?

HOW TO WRITE LIKE A BOSS

Ben here. As you begin this book we encourage you to read with a growth mindset. Writing is a calling that compels us to create, but writing Like a Boss is so much more. The purpose of this book is to blend your talent with a foundation of business, because both are required to forge a career. Throughout this book we're going to talk about things like word count, mindset, and goals, all of which may be foreign to your inner artist. The business of writing does not impede the art of creation, and in fact it expands your ability to connect with an audience. In short, the topics of this book are meant to augment your craft.

Whether you have two books or twenty, we want to encourage and inspire you to grow as a writer and as a business owner. Many writers (including myself!) struggled with motivation and a lack of industry knowledge early in their careers. The learning curve has only gotten steeper with the advent of e-publishing, and it's more important than ever that we as writers push ourselves into the modern world of publishing. You know how to write. Now let's Write Like a Boss.

Honorée here. What's the difference between the full-time writer and someone who wants to be a full-time writer? We're glad you asked!

In our minds, the difference is clear, and we've written this book to help you make the hop, skip, or jump from *I want to be a full-timer* to *Yes, sir, I am a full-time writer!*

The first step in your process from side hustle to full-time gig, from part-time to full-time, begins and ends with *writing like a boss*. The other books in the Series, *Publish Like a Boss,* and *Market Like a Boss,* will tell you just about everything you need to know. For right now, we know for sure your writing game has got to be tight, and that is our focus here!

Who are we? We are both full-time writers with more than 50 books under our belts and the six-figure annual incomes that go along with them.

We're writing this book together for a few reasons: one, we each think the other person is awesome! (It's true, she's awesome.) Two, we admire each other and our respective careers. And three, and this is all about you, dear reader—we want to help you!

The questions we get on a regular basis are all around one question (*How can I become a full-time writer?*) that can be answered with the contents of these three books.

We know it takes a combination of consistent production, the ability to treat your writing like a product, a keen eye for what's working (and not working), and so much more!

Honorée is correct. Your talent for writing does not hone itself, and in this book, we'll teach you how to turn your talent into a profession. The truth is that writing full-time is *much* more than just writing. It's understanding yourself, how you write, how you outline, and so much more. Someone coined the term "life hacks" to describe surprisingly simple things that make your life easier. Well, here we're going to teach you the "self-hacks" which will help you learn how to master yourself. Once you do, the publishing world is just waiting for a new conqueror.

Throughout this book you'll see two fonts, each representing our distinct voices. I write fiction and Honorée writes nonfiction. We have many similarities in our disciplines but a few distinctions as well. Between the two of us we have a great deal of experience in writing and publishing. As you join us in this conversation, keep in mind that not everything will apply to you, and that's okay. Writing is highly unique for every individual, so what works for you may not work for someone else.

What's important is that you study this book with an eye for what you lack. Decades worth of knowledge from two full-time writers are contained within these pages, and I'm confident you will find exactly what you are searching for. The dream of writing full-time doesn't have to be your dream. It can be your reality.

First, we're going to tackle writing—because that's where it all begins, right? Because seriously, if you don't write, you don't write. No writing, no words. No words, no books.

We suggest you grab a blank journal and keep it handy while you read—we have lots of fun exercises for you to do that will help you *Write Like a Boss.*

So, let's get down to it.

MINDSET:

FROM HOBBY TO BUSINESS

I'm going to start because mindset is my jam. In every book I write, I always begin with a little something about mindset because, by gosh and by golly, if you don't have your mind right, nothing else is going to fall into place.

But if you're thinking of skipping this section because you think you've read everything there is on mindset, or because you don't believe mindset is important, in a word, *don't*.

Why? Because you're only going to be able to progress as far as your mind will take you. Now I've got lots to say about this in *The Prosperous Writer Mindset* (just about everything), so you'll only have to stay with me for a few pages here—but these few pages can help you crush your writing goals! If you skip them, you might be like a bag of discarded puppies on the side of the road. And that's just wrong.

The *one thing* you must do to write like a boss is shift your mindset from that of a writing hobbyist to that of a writing professional.

A hobbyist thinks it would be fun to write a book (maybe two), and thinks a lot about writing. They have a book they want to write, and without a care in the world or any form of intention or purpose, sit down and just start writing. They talk constantly about the book they want to write, and even contemplate taking some time (perhaps a week from Thursday would be delightful) to start writing.

Sometimes they even publish their work. Their finished manuscript is the amalgamation of a few dozen thoughts, or perhaps some cobbled together blog posts. They might even find some success with a book, two, or three, but there's no intention or purpose attached to their writing or their writing business.

Honorée is perfectly on point. If you treat your writing like a hobby, it's unlikely to ever be anything more. To be clear, if you only want to write one book that's not a bad thing. Writing is an incredible hobby regardless of what you write. If that's your goal, you'll still find a lot of value in this book because its purpose is to help you write smarter, faster, and better.

However, if you want to be a full-time, six-figure, loving-your-job-and-life writer, your mindset makes all the difference in the world. I love to snowboard and know that if I really wanted to, I could snowboard as a profession. But that's not the life I want. (I think!) I treat snowboarding like a hobby and I'm happy with that.

When I started writing I *wanted* it to be a career. At the time I had three children (I now have six) and I wanted as much time with my family as possible. The idea of having a career I would love and that also gave me time sounded like an impossible dream. To me it would have been like my five-foot-ten, white-guy-with-white-guy-jumping-skills personage getting into the NBA. Yeah, never going to happen. Do you feel that way? That having a career in writing is impossible? Well that's the way I felt.

But it didn't matter, I believed I could make it happen. I treated it like a business and invested $5,000 into my books before I published my first.

You may be thinking that what I did was foolish, that I was throwing money down a well. But I was investing into myself, because I believed in myself. I've met authors that want to write full-time but don't plan beyond a hobby. Don't make the mistake of wanting more while planning for less.

I won't lie to you, the business of writing is hard, and passion for the craft is rarely enough to carry you to your dream. It requires diligence, learning, adaptation, and the will to change yourself. But before you can change yourself you have to change your perspective. If you view your books as a hobby they will never be anything more.

Treat your books like the business they will become, and your books will become your business.

If you do view your writing as a hobby, you'll wander aimlessly, wondering why you aren't more successful and wishing you were. I understand completely!

Lest you think we are sitting up here on our writer thrones, wearing the garb of 17th century royalty and judging the hobbyist, you couldn't be more wrong. In fact, we see hobbyist behavior in many who could sit alongside us at the cool kids' table (just kidding) with a few key distinctions combined with some simple behavior shifts.

Ben and I want you to treat your writing like a business so you can reap all the rewards! Imagine making a living from your writing (and giving up whatever it is you do now—assuming you don't also love it), writing the guidebooks or stories you spend hours contemplating.

And we're not talking a month-to-month, that poor writer looks like he *could* be homeless, kind of living. We're talking about the kind of living that affords you a wonderful place to live, driving a car you love, and even enough left over to take regular vacations (a.k.a. trips to fabulous places that inspire more writing).

The journey from where you are now to your vision of bliss is going to take work, there's no question! In the pages of this book, you'll learn everything you need to know to formulate your plan, figure out what you need to do on a consistent basis, and learn how to write like a boss.

From Vision to Reality in Four Easy Steps

If you find the mental shift from hobbyist to professional daunting, I have great news! You can make the transition. Let's start with four easy steps.

1. **Decide what you want.** I know, I know. It always starts with a decision. Which you might be reticent to make, considering somewhere in your mind you might think you'll fail. As a wise man once said, *The past doesn't equal the future.* All you have to do, and I mean it, it's this simple, is to make the decision you want what you want. Go ahead, say it: *I want to ....* Now, grab a piece of paper, a Post-It, or a napkin (it doesn't really matter right now), and write your declaration down.

   This is more important than you might realize. Writing down what you want makes it real—it takes the intangible and makes it tangible. Posting it makes you feel accountable. A thought can be ignored, but a paper demands attention. Don't let your goals remain unwritten.

   We're not kidding. We'll wait. Grab your journal and write it down!

2. **Define what it takes to have it.** Defining what it takes is a little harder than step #1. Most of the rest of this book gives you the "how to" for your writing business. In the coming pages, you'll be able to define the best course of action to reach your desired outcome. Grab a highlighter to go with

your now not-blank journal so you can capture your thoughts, ideas, and inspirations along the way.

This part has auxiliary benefits that you may not expect. Part of becoming a full-time writer is learning how to open a conduit between thoughts and paper. The biggest hallmark of professional writers is not marketing skills or business knowledge, it is consistency. Every time you write an idea down, you open that conduit. Ignore an idea and you close it down. Whether you use it or not, get it onto paper. Open that conduit until it becomes a flood. Then ride the wave.

3. **Deliberately affirm you can do it!** You might be tempted to underestimate the power of self-talk. But, I can assure you that what you say when you talk to yourself can be the difference between *I did it* and *I'm still not a full-time writer.* Take your declaration from number one (above) and turn it into an affirmation you think and say, oh, about a zillion times every day. If your declaration is *I want to be a full-time fiction writer earning in excess of $100,000 a year*, turn that into *I AM a full-time, six-figure fiction author and I love it!*

You'll say it so often that the next time you're at a cocktail party you might have to stop yourself from saying your affirmation, because, at least for the time being, you're still a middle school science teacher.

4. **Refuse to doubt.** For writers, discouragement and doubt are constants. Whether you have two books or twenty, you will inevitably face the insidious voice that tells you aren't good enough, you aren't smart enough, your life is too hard, your dreams are too big. This is where you begin to find your writing courage. Let me say it right here. You are good enough. You are smart enough. Your life is hard but that won't stop you. Your dreams will never be big enough. Be relentless. Be undaunted. Be a writer.

Four easy steps will take you from where you are to writing like a boss. Seems too easy, right? Well, let me tell you something amazing (like so amazing that, when I got it, it changed my life forever and ever and it's why I'm able to write this book for you)! *You cannot affirm something over and over and not eventually bring it into being.*

Our beliefs, the ones that live deep down in our subconscious mind—the same ones formed when we were too young to understand what was happening—drive our behavior and determine our reality. So, it might sound like our course is set. And it is, until we discover there's a way to take those beliefs and change them, all the while installing new beliefs that cause us to act automatically in the exact way we want.

In short, everyone grows up believing a lot of things—yet few believe in themselves. This is where you change that. Because achieving *any* dream requires discipline, effort, and sacrifice. Why go through all that? Why did Honorée and I go through all that? Because we LOVE our jobs. More importantly, we LOVE our lives. (Amen to that!)

I love my wife, my kids, the church I attend, my friends, all of it. All came with a price. I didn't get my life because I waited for it to come, I have my life because I willed it into being—not because I deserved it (we all deserve a happy life), but because I was willing to do what it took to *make it happen*. If you don't believe in yourself, you're in luck, because that's where everyone starts.

When I wrote my first book I didn't tell anyone for two years—because I didn't believe anyone would like it. I had to build my confidence one tiny fragment at a time, forge my writing courage until I could not just tell people about my book, but publish it and endure the readers' scathing critique.

Are you starting to see the pattern? We start with a vision and a desire, and then we push our desire toward our vision. It's the pattern for writing and life, but the roadmap from desire to vision is unique for each of us. Fortunately, this book should help you build your roadmap.

What are we talking about? We're talking about the easy way to get yourself to write like a boss: the repetition of your affirmation. You see, you absolutely 100 percent cannot say something to yourself over and over, such as, *I write a thousand words every day*, without eventually doing that exact thing.

Studies have shown just how powerful our brains are, and when we talk to ourselves, the truth must be told. When you identify a behavior you want to change, or an outcome you want to bring about, and start saying it via an affirmation, one of two things will happen. You will either:

1. Stop saying it, or

2. Start doing it.

It could take a few days or several months. Behavioral changes and results are rarely instantaneous (sorry about that!), yet if you keep your faith and keep doing the affirmation, sooner or later you'll find yourself with the result you want, or engaged in the behavior you've been affirming.

Here's an example:

Every day, I say my vision statement. It consists of affirmations to support my goals, which are based on my bigger life vision. I decided to experiment with a few affirmations, to see if they truly worked. I started affirming *I study French every single day*. At the time, I wasn't consistent with my studies, not even close. I was doing what most writers do: I was thinking an awful lot about French, daydreaming about how wonderful it would be to hold an entire conversation *en français* with the lady from Paris who runs a bakery five minutes from where I live. But not studying French.

Then I realized I could test what I had learned about my brain being a super computer I could program. I began an experiment: every day, I would affirm *I study French every single day*. It was almost ironic for a few weeks as I would affirm *I study French every day* and then … not do it.

But I started to notice shirts people were wearing with French words on them. My author buddy Brian Meeks told me about Memrise (an app that teaches different topics in a very cool way). "Out of the blue" I decided to use my Audible credits to buy Pimsleur French I and II (sixty lessons!). I even discovered a French coach in Paris and started taking her class. One evening as I was reading my affirmation *I study French every single day*, I realized I-was-studying-French-every-single-day. It just kind of snuck up on me!

I thought back to the transition from not studying to studying—it all began with the affirmation. Then, I started writing it on my daily to-do list in my Bullet Journal. As part of a fitness challenge that required double workouts, I realized I could listen to verb drills while I was getting my 10,000 steps in on the treadmill. I found I could do a little French lesson while I was cooling my jets at a coffee shop, waiting for someone to arrive. In other words, my subconscious mind "got right on it" and started ensuring my French studies got done.

But before we dive in further, Ben has a few words about his mindset journey I know you'll want to hear:

I shared a little of my story earlier, but here I'd like to share a little more. And it didn't begin with pen and paper.

When I was young my mom was frequently sick. (She's better now!) Because of this I spent a lot of time with my dad, who had grown up on a farm. He believed

I should work like I grew up on a farm, even though we grew up in a suburban neighborhood. Long story short, I had a full-time job in the summer of my seventh grade year. I also typically worked three days a week after school and nearly every Saturday. On top of that I did a lot of chores at home—cooking, cleaning, and my own laundry.

I enjoyed spending so much time with my dad and brothers but loathed working so hard. On one occasion my dad caught me taking a nap on the job. (I was around 10 years old.) He promptly fired me. Elated, I exclaimed, "So I don't have to work anymore?"

He said, "Yes you do, but you no longer get paid."

It took me two weeks before I earned back my wage.

Sounds intense, right? It was. I didn't realize until later that my dad was teaching me how life worked. Accomplishment requires hard work. But what is hard work? It's focus and consistent effort. It's rarely fast, it's not often pretty, but it continues because you don't stop. You keep working and learning and growing, until suddenly the job is done.

Every time I said I couldn't do something, he would respond, "So you need to learn." I hated that phrase, because it meant I had to do something I didn't want to. Now it means everything to me.

You might be thinking, what does any of this have to do with writing? It has everything to do with writing. When I was 25 I began writing, a task which I thought was *outside my ability*. But I *knew* I could learn it. Amid all

11

the hours of construction with my dad, I'd learned that I was *capable of anything*. I wasn't limited by my ability or situation, those were merely obstacles. (Of which there have been many!) My only limitation was doubt. And my dad taught me to believe in myself.

At twenty-five I started writing and learning. I worked hard to master a skill I'd never even tried. It took years, countless hours, and sacrifice to attain the mediocre talent I currently think I possess. That's not being humble, I just think there is so much more for me to learn. My dad taught me to master myself. Now I can master writing. See what I did there? I described my mindset, and how it became the foundation for my career. If you haven't already, start with what you do believe. It won't matter how much you learn if you don't believe you can apply it in your writing. Have you set your mindset yet? Good. Then your foundation is placed. Let's build your career!

It's Your Turn

What is your *I am* statement? What do you want to declare for yourself, even if you can't see a way at this moment for it to come into being? Step out in faith and make your declaration. Grab your journal and write it down. Memorize it. Think it and say it. We're right here cheering you on!

Now that you've made that all-important declaration, let's get down to business!

2

THIS IS YOUR
BUSINESS!

Writers are a special breed of people. We are able to take our thoughts and put them down on paper (at least in theory). Many people struggle with what we take for granted—words flowing from our fingertips as we turn the moving pictures of our minds into words on a page.

What starts as a hobby when we are kids can turn into a full-time career. I've listened to many individuals share how they started writing stories during boring classes as early as elementary school, and daydreaming about one day becoming a novelist.

Then, in college, they would take a journalism or even creative writing degree. They tried not to listen to their parents give chapter and verse about the dangers of becoming a "starving artist," all while begging them to do something more practical with their lives (something fun and more fruitful like law school).

And there is absolutely nothing wrong with being practical (I'm known for being practical myself), or engaging in a career that will put bread on the table. But listen up! If you want to be a full-time writer, *you can*. There's some work you're going to have to do (oh, is there!), and there are mental shifts (some subtle, some gigantic) you must make. Finally, there's a commitment you have to make that is not unlike the commitment you would make, or even have made, to any other career.

As traditional publishing has become more and more difficult to break into, and self-publishing easier to navigate, the opportunity to live your dream of being a full-time writer has never been more possible.

The Decision

The sole purpose of this book is to help you make the transition from *I want to be a full-time writer* to *I AM a full-time writer.* Ben and I can and do share every aspect of what it takes to create a successful writing business. Ultimately, though, your success comes down to one pivotal moment: the moment you decide you must be a full-time writer, there is no other option, and you're willing to do what it takes, for as long as it takes, to be a full-time writer.

I must caution you that it is critical you make your decision with one hundred percent certainty. Without question, there are easier and faster ways to make a living. I have found any worthwhile endeavor always takes longer, costs more money, and requires much more effort than originally thought. When we set off in pursuit of our goals, we're convinced our enthusiasm is enough to make it happen "in a jiffy." Keep in mind, it may take you years to become as successful and prosperous a writer as you desire in this moment. How is that different than any other career? (It isn't.)

You have to start looking at professional writing as a small business. You are just like any other entrepreneur. Your business creates products which you market and sell over the Internet, you have a website so your customers can find you, and you work hard to develop a brand your customers will be loyal to. When you make this perspective shift from writer to entrepreneur, you'll see your career in the right light. Like any other small business, writing is hard and requires full commitment. The good news is that if you have a passion for the craft, the business is the most rewarding you can imagine.

Like any small business, a big reason why one is successful versus another is commitment. Committed writers work extra hours while they have their regular job, writing consistently despite the distractions of life. When I first started writing I had three kids and a different small business. Finding time to write was HARD. But I was committed to it. When I started writing full-time I maintained my commitment, and continuously wrote every day.

Consistent writing is the product of your commitment. An author that writes an average of 500 words day (five days a week) for ten years will produce an astonishing 1.8 *million* words.

If you want to dream big, make a big commitment. The height of your success will not be determined by luck, where one special reader finds your book and *then* you have it made. It will be determined by your daily commitment to your goal.

Commitment is an interesting thing, because it changes our very natures. Our entire history is littered with evidence of people who have done the impossible because they were committed. The list of writers who have done the impossible is longer than this book, but not one of them was successful in a single day. It is the daily commitment that changes your nature, helping you rise from amateur to professional.

Committing fully to your desired outcome will serve you well when you're offered less for an article than you think it is worth, or you launch a book and it doesn't sell right away. Or you must renew the lease on your one bedroom apartment in a less-than-stellar part of town for one more year while you bang away on your laptop, day in and day out. Or you know you must put up with your cranky boss for a few more months until you have enough money in reserve to sustain a budding writing career.

I understand!

Your challenge will be, as it has been for me, to maintain the level of commitment for the desired outcome long after the initial enthusiasm has worn off.

You know, deep down in your soul, you were born to be a writer. You have stories to tell, words to write, and you cannot quell that desire any longer. Aren't you ready to commit? I thought so…

What's the decision you want to make right now? To quit your full-time job within a year and write full-time? To publish your long-overdue novel by Christmas? Great! You made your declaration, now make your commitment. To yourself, to your writing business, to whomever or whatever else needs to be included.

Write it down, right under your declaration (be sure to put it in your journal so you always know where it is), and let's continue.

The Commitment

It's been a long time since I've put a commitment to a goal in writing, yet just like writing and saying your daily *I am* statement, the technique of writing down what you're committed to works wonders for achieving results.

You might have a little voice in your head, immediately following your affirmation.

- *I am a full-time writer.*
- *No, you're not.*

- *I am a full-time writer.*

- *No, you're not, and you won't ever be.*

This mini-argument might go on for a little while. One way to put it to rest is to also write what you're committed to *doing*.

You want to be a writer? You must write every day. Professional writers and successful authors follow a production schedule based on their book business plan (more on that soon). *I am a writer* is paired nicely with *I write two thousand words every day (like a boss)*. You might have just laughed out loud at that number, I mean *two thousand words? Really?* Yes. Ben's goal is 3,500 words every day, my goal is 2,500 words every day (I'm clearly the slacker of this pair). We've committed to our writing businesses, and we put our butts in seats every day and write.

This point goes back to what I talked about earlier about a conduit. Imagine your creativity like a spigot of water. The more you use your creativity, the more words flow out. You have to get used to a constant flow of words to paper. The more you practice, the easier it flows, and more water comes out of the spigot.

This can go both ways. The *less* you write, the harder it becomes to write. This can prove to be a challenge when life throws you a curve. Injuries, losses of loved ones, problems with a spouse, money, or any other situation can leave you with a weight that stifles your creativity. As hard as they are, all of these are part of normal life. Taking a break from writing to deal with a crisis is fine, of course, but don't let it become a habit. Once that occurs, your spigot is shut off and it can become really hard to write again.

The trick to overcoming this is to *use* what is happening in your life to continue writing. These are the same events your readers are going through, so incorporating your own struggles into fictional characters will make them more relatable. Keeping your writing commitment is about threading it into your life, not adding it to your already busy life.

We watch new writers start with more modest writing goals, just as we did ourselves. If you work full-time, go to school, and are training for a marathon—all while clutching tightly to the dream of being a writer—it's perfectly fine to set a daily writing target goal of one hundred or even two hundred words a day.

While just a couple of hundred words a day seems small, let's talk about what happens when you stick to it. Over the course of a year, writing weekdays only (two hundred and fifty days, total), you'll crank out an impressive fifty thousand words! And, that, kids, is a robust nonfiction book or a darned good start to a novel! If you can find it possible to raise your goal to three hundred words a day, just five days a week, in a year's time you'll have seventy-five thousand words. *Two* nonfiction books or one nice-sized novel. Not too shabby!

You know what you need to do: make a commitment to the number of words you're going to write every day. Keep it simple, almost easy, and completely doable. I even have a book that can help you develop a daily writing habit, *The Nifty 15: Write Your Book in Just 15 Minutes a Day* (Book 2, The Prosperous Writer Series).

Thank you for referencing that book. (You're welcome!) If you hadn't, I would have. When I started out I had a really hard time because I didn't know what I was doing. I wrote when I could but I was reinventing the wheel, so to speak. Everything from writing to editing and marketing I had to learn from scratch. Having a how-to guide would have saved me *months* of mistakes. Don't hesitate to get help.

If you've followed instructions to this point, you've now made a declaration, penned a decision, and made a commitment to your writing business. These are three important pieces in the bigger picture of your writing business. So far, so good.

The Learning Curve & Your Productivity Progress

I alluded to the possibility that you could write full-time, and a full-time writer writes and writes and writes—thousands of words a day. Mat Morris wrote an astounding fifty thousand words in a day. Our friend Julie Huss routinely writes upwards of ten thousand words a day. We regularly write thousands of words every day on our various WIPs (works-in-progress).

I guarantee you that none of us started out with word counts even close to that. My first writing consisted of blog posts ranging from two hundred to five hundred words (written over several days). Ben started his writing career by also setting a goal…

In my first year of writing my goal was 500 words a day, and I didn't reach it. I had three kids and a small business, and time was very tight. The next year I set the same goal, and this time I did reach it. Then I went for a 1,000. It's not the word count that matters, it's the consistency! The hallmark of a professional writer is consistency, so start where you already are. Write *every day*. Set a goal—even if it's just 100 words—and then stick to it. When you think it's getting easy, push it. Don't compare yourself to someone's 10,000 words a day, compare yourself to you! Are you writing more than last year? Five years ago? If you are, you're doing great! If not, examine what in your life makes it hard and make small changes for a big impact.

You'll have a learning curve that will coincide with a natural increase in your productivity. As you learn more about developing your writing business, you'll increase the amount of words you're able to produce on a consistent basis.

Similarly, when going from couch potato to marathon runner, the first day you undergo a fitness challenge you don't eat lean meats, drink a gallon of water, and run ten miles. You go for a twenty-minute walk (which is exhausting), try to drink more water, and maybe add a side salad to dinner. Over time, you get leaner, stronger, and more confident until eventually you are healthy and fit and inspiring others to turn off the tube and don some running shoes.

You will notice incremental increases in your own confidence when it comes to writing—the more you write, the more you write. You'll build your writing muscles and easily crank out a word count that today might seem impossible. (Keep in mind that the word "impossible" indeed means "I'm possible.")

When I started writing full-time I noticed an adverse side effect that no one warned me about—weight gain. I began to see the scale reach numbers I'd never seen, and at one point I balked. I realized I had to make small changes now or I'd be the size of a buffalo. My first rule?

No brownies for breakfast. (I mean, only a guy would even do that!)

I'm fairly fit and athletic, but this was hard for me! It sounds stupid, but it was *really* hard. This tiny change gave me the courage to make another change, which brought me to rule #2.

No brownies for lunch. (Eye roll!)

You can see where this is going. Writing is the same way. Make a small change, such as "I will write 100 words before going to bed." (See the declaration!) One change leads to another, and another. I can trace my entire career to a single idea I had when I was young. Small changes add up. Small word counts add up.

But the true strength in consistency is not the big results it builds, it's the habit it creates. Previously I talked about how 500 words a day over a decade is 1.8 million words. However, how long before the 500 words becomes easy? What about 1,000? 2,000? I've been writing full-time for nearly five years, and my daily word count is approaching the 5,000 word mark. I'm just starting a decade where I plan to average 5,000 words per day. If 500 words per day is 1.3 million words, then what is 5,000?

It's an unbelievable 13,000,000 words! That's the power of consistency.

With the expectation that you'll get better and better the more and longer you write, it will be helpful for you to have a solid plan for your writing business.

Your Full-time Writer Action Plan

Flourishing full-time writers, like any successful professionals, work from a business plan. The business plan consists of:

- A vision statement, also known as a version of your *I am* statement

- A purpose statement

- Specific, measurable goals

- Identified action steps

Your Vision Statement

Your vision statement, otherwise known as "what you want," is the clear picture you hold in your mind of what you want your writing business ultimately to become. I love thinking about the time when I will have hundreds of books published, and that the readers of those books are either inspired (nonfiction) or entertained (fiction), while I earn more than enough to travel the world and write books in amazing locations and cozy coffee shops.

What is the picture you have in your mind for your writing? Take a few moments (or hours, if you'd like, after all, you're a writer and it might take some time and lots of words) and turn the picture you have in your mind's eye to words in your journal.

Your Purpose Statement

Your purpose statement, also known as "why you want the what," contains the reasons you want to bring your vision to fruition. It is a breeze to begin a project with vim and vigor and race to the finish line strong and fierce when we can finally see it. As I said earlier, it is challenging to maintain the same levels of enthusiasm and commitment in what I affectionately call the "yucky middle." In the middle, we are prone to being sidetracked or sidelined by any number of opposing forces, internal or external. These forces take the form of illnesses, our families, vacations, holidays, unexpected projects—the list goes on and on. A purpose statement with strong emotional language to connect us to why we attempted this venture in the first place can keep us focused and moving forward as we face the drudgery of completing our daily tasks, tackle an unexpected challenge, or wonder why we started in the first place.

Now would be a terrific time to ink a few paragraphs about why you want to be a full-time writer. What will it give you? What will a career as a writer allow you to do? Where will you be able to go? Who will you get a chance to meet or get to know? What will it provide for your personal growth, for your family, for the world? Don't worry, you don't have to publish it or allow anyone else to see it. This statement is for you and you alone, and you get to make it as simple or as grandiose as your heart desires.

I like to think of the vision as the dream, the purpose as the destination. The purpose statement should contain specific statements that answer the questions Honorée mentioned. For example, saying "I want financial freedom" is good, but "I want to earn $100,000 a year" is better. One is ambiguous and difficult to measure, while the other is clear and easy to measure. The purpose statement does not need to be large, just enough that you have a clear idea of your game plan. Don't make the mistake of skipping this step because you "know" your purpose. You cannot reach the vision without having a plan to get there. These statements give you a destination in mind which will keep you focused on what you want, and as we've mentioned, life has a way of making us lose our focus. Write your purpose down and you are ready for your next step.

Your Goals and Desired Outcomes

As we get into the detail of goals, think of these goals as stepping stones to reach your vision and purpose statement. Many aspiring writers compare themselves to a big name, but doing so is a mistake. They are years into their goals and have probably already achieved their first vision and moved on to their second, third, or tenth. Goals are like little stepping stones, each a measurable destination that goes where you want to go. That part is important. I've met authors that want to write full-time but write in multiple genres, use different pen names, and join anthologies. Each of these require their own goals, but they actually move in different directions. I've been invited to participate in several writing projects. When I have, I pulled out my list of goals to see if the project lined up. Would they have been fun? Certainly. Would I have grown as a writer? Of course! Did they align with my goals? Unfortunately not. They would have been stepping stones toward a different vision! I turned them down so I could stay focused, and that has led me to move in the right direction. (I'm glad I got to be the lucky collaborator!)

Vision and purpose statements are terrific at keeping us mentally focused, especially when we review them daily (hint). I write my commitment statements on a 3x5 card *every single morning* and review them several times a day. I keep mine in my Bullet Journal, which I reference a dozen times each day. Each time I open my journal, I see my commitment card and take fifteen seconds to read it.

The next very important piece of the puzzle is to set goals. While sometimes looked upon as old-fashioned, I still advocate for SMART goals for several reasons (not the least of which: *they work!*).

Specific

Manageable

Action-oriented

Risky

Time-sensitive goals

Allow me to explain these in depth and the reasoning behind each one.

Specific.

You might want to "lose some weight." But if you step on the scale tomorrow and you're down .2 pounds, I'm sure that's not exactly what you had in mind. A specific goal is key because you either achieve it or you don't. You either write and publish your novel by December 15th, or you don't. The goal to "write and publish my novel" isn't specific enough, because there's no deadline. To go one step further, a specific goal could be *to write three hundred words every weekday and complete the first draft of my novel by September 1st*. Very specific. You'll know if the goal has either been achieved or not, and anyone watching would know as well.

Setting specific goals can be a challenge sometimes, because it's a very ambiguous idea. For example, "learn marketing" is a decent goal but there is no way to cross it off the list. "Study marketing 30 minutes a day for six months" is a much more specific goal. Like Honorée said, you either complete it or you don't. A nonspecific goal might linger on your list of goals until you start to avoid it because it can never be completed.

Manageable.

It is key to keep your goals manageable, in other words, you should feel like you can "manage to get them accomplished." Despite all your other obligations, attention must be paid to your goal on a consistent

WRITE LIKE A BOSS

basis. If you feel as though it is too ambitious or time-consuming, you'll quickly lose hope it can be achieved and are likely to abandon it altogether. When setting your goal, there is a key piece at play: you must always look for the opportunities and possibilities to work on your goal (as opposed to finding reasons or excuses why you can't). Your goals will be manageable to the extent you always come from a place of intention and purpose. This is my mantra, it might work for you as well: *I will get this done no matter what!*

Action-Oriented.

What are the actions you must take to achieve your goal? I've alluded to a daily word count, and without question, this is a key component. There are other actions needed to accomplish your goal, and they must be identified, agreed to, and put on the calendar!

Action-oriented goals aren't just a destination ("by December 6th") but a means to reach the destination ("write 625 words a day to finish by December 6th"). Making a goal that's just a destination is like saying you'll go to Hawaii without ever planning how to pay for it. You want to go to Hawaii, don't you?! I thought so. We'll see you there! Aloha!

Risky.

This is my favorite goal-setting criteria of the bunch, because when I set a goal that is, by my standards, *risky*, I always get my performance to a level I perhaps didn't believe was possible.

I don't mean risky as in "you (or someone else) could be harmed." I mean it in the sense that you know it's a risk to set your sights so high, to attempt something seemingly out of reach.

My first year of writing full-time was not what I expected. Four months into the year my sales plummeted and although I'd prepared for it, I faced the real possibility of having to quit writing full-time. I did manage to finish my first book in five months and had seven months left in the year. This gave me a choice, should I write one book and finish with two months to spare? Or go for two books? I set the risky goal of writing two books in seven months (each book was about 100,000 words). I wasn't sure I could do it but I was committed and published the third book on December 22nd. I did it, but more importantly the next year I *started* thinking I could do three books. Because of my risky goal, I managed to keep my readership going and kept writing full-time. Setting risky goals is about stretching yourself, and what was once hard gradually becomes easy. Make sure your goals are attainable but risky, and then watch yourself soar.

Consider this: it might be beneath your pay grade to write one hundred words per day, when you're capable of so much more. I always ask myself these questions: *What am I truly capable of? How good could this get?* There is such a thing as a goal that is too ambitious, so lofty it takes all the fun out of achieving it. It might not be even remotely possible. This type of goal causes one to lose hope, and this isn't the idea at all. In other words, avoid setting the goal of writing twelve books your first year, if you haven't written your first book. You could set the goal of writing your first draft in ninety days, with the idea you could write two books in twelve months.

Here's how you know you have the right goal: if it makes you a little nauseous because you know you're going to have to focus as never before, and give it your all *and you feel with extraordinary effort you can achieve it*, **this is the right goal.** I promise!

Time-sensitive.

A goal with a deadline is a goal that gets attention, and more times than not, gets achieved. You must have a deadline, dare I say *aggressive deadline*, on your goals. Why? Because the time you give yourself to do something is the time you take to do it. I've been given seven days to write my portion of this book, about fifteen thousand words in all, or 2,143 per day. Before I said yes, I knew I was already fully committed but I said *YES!* anyway. Why? Because this book, and those who will read it and benefit from it, were important enough for me to find the time to crank out my daily word count.

I originally had an appointment scheduled at the time I'm writing this. When the person asked to reschedule, I jumped at the chance and immediately committed to *write more words.* No harm in finishing ahead of the deadline, right?

Honorée didn't tell me this when we scheduled the writing of this book. She just said, "I can do it." And I didn't doubt it because her confidence is undeniable.

On my end, I committed to write this book when I had my own challenges. I was already writing 3,000 words a day in my fantasy series, as well as spending an hour a day on my Master's Program. On top of all that I was committed to ending work at 4:00 every day so I could spend extra time with my family.

In short, I was already writing 3,500 words a day between my job and school, and doing it all in seven hours. To commit to this book, I would have to increase my word count to 5,000 words per day, adding significantly to my word count goal. What did I say? *I can do it.* I'm currently on my second read-through of this book and I am on pace to finish on time. I set a time-sensitive goal and stuck to it, and I won't let anything stop me from finishing on time. This principle is essential in goal making, and I use it every single day.

Close Your Gap

By completing **Your Full-Time Writer Action Plan**, you have identified what we call "the gap." The gap is the space between where you are now, budding full-time writer, and full-time writer.

You might be wondering what we advise to close the gap, and we're glad you asked. While Ben and I work a little differently, there are enough similarities between our approaches that we know the principles we share are valid.

With **Your Full-Time Writer Action Plan** in place, you will want to define three other key pieces of the plan: the production schedule (to ensure you write and produce the requisite number of products to support your financial goals), the marketing schedule, and the rest of your time.

Let's begin with your **Production Schedule.**

At the beginning of each year, I define the number of books I want to write that year and ensure my daily word count supports my goals. Each book, in my case, nonfiction, runs around 35,000 words. With a daily production schedule of 2,000 words, I can complete a final first-draft manuscript in about eighteen days.

I work from a detailed outline, which generally takes me three to four hours to complete. Once the outline is finished, I'm all set to start writing.

Writing six days a week, I can finish a first-draft within three weeks. Some books are longer, others are shorter. But at two thousand words a day, six days a week, I can easily write twelve nonfiction books each year.

The next step is to marry my production schedule with the books I want to write, organizing them according to my priorities, and finally adding them to my calendar. Since I can write two thousand words in less than ninety minutes a day, it is sufficient for me to schedule my writing time from 6-7:30 a.m. Monday through Saturday to stay on schedule.

Since I don't want to be on a tight deadline *all the time*, I generally shoot for six to eight books a year, which allows me the time to fit in extra projects, capitalize on opportunities as they come up (a quick trip to Nashville to watch the Predators compete for the Stanley Cup? Yes, please! Deliver a keynote presentation with less than a month's notice for a premium fee? You betcha!), and enjoy some down time to recharge my batteries. More on that later, but first, let's hear from Ben.

I also start the year by defining what I want to write, and then I break it into weekly and daily goals. My purpose statement is for the year, my goals are weekly and daily. This year my goal was to write 3,500 words every day. I write 3,000 words on my fantasy novel, which equates to a first draft of my 100,000-word novel in just six weeks. Then I write a minimum of 500 words to my master's degree. I started the year struggling to hit that mark, but now I'm averaging 3,900 words. So, let's look at the math. Six weeks to write a novel, so eighteen weeks to write three. My editing process is another five weeks. (I'll get into the draft process later.) So, to edit my three fantasy books is another fifteen weeks (just over four months to finish my fantasy novels for the year. That's thirty-three weeks total, with nineteen weeks left in the year.)

Now, this is where I do things differently than most. I also allocate my time to other things. I block out five weeks for personal time. This applies to holidays, sick days, vacations, etc. Because I block this out at the beginning of the year, it frees me from the weight of deadlines. I can take a day off because I planned for it. I also block out two weeks of conference time, a mainstay of full-time writers. This frees me from feeling like I have to write when I go to a conference. I also block out three weeks of outlining time throughout the year. (I am a HUGE plotter!)

If you're keeping track, that brings my total of planned weeks to forty-three weeks, leaving nine weeks. This year I plan on writing a fourth book! Remember earlier when I struggled to just write three books? Each year I've set higher goals and pushed myself to achieve them. In December, I will have been writing full-time for five years, and I keep pushing myself forward.

What I want you to get out of this is not the output, it's the consistency. I set an average and stuck to it. You know what my writing goal was before I wrote full-time? Just 500 words a day. And it was *hard*. Now my writing goals are light years ahead of what they were originally, I'm in a Master's Program, and I now have six kids. Think your life is chaos? Trust me, I know the feeling. The point is that goals make a *massive* impact on achievement. If your goal is 10,000 words or just ten, it doesn't matter. Set it. Maintain it. Push it.

Next, your **Marketing Schedule.**

You may be asking why we would put a marketing schedule into a book on writing, so let's talk about why it's important. When you write to a market you are probably making certain assumptions about that market. It's a prerequisite. However, those very assumptions create the basis to your future marketing efforts. You are defining your market of readers—and they are your customers. If you begin your preliminary marketing plans even before you've written the book, you'll be able to hone your book to target your desired market. If not, you may end up struggling to market a book to a market that isn't exactly what you thought.

Let's use an example. Let's pretend you want to write a dark fantasy and DON'T plan your marketing at the same time. The story is incredible, driven and detailed, exciting and shocking. But because this author didn't review his target, he makes two critical mistakes.

Mistake number one: The market is much smaller than this author anticipated, so despite their best efforts, the book has little room to grow.

Mistake number two: The book doesn't quite fit in with many of the other books within the genre, so readers don't quite click with it.

By the time the author realizes the error it is too late, their book has several negative reviews because it wasn't what the readers expected. And the book is already written so they can't change genres.

The above example illustrates how preliminary marketing efforts will actually help you **shape your book** to better target your market. This isn't a huge change, but in the world of publishing, small changes add up to big ones.

There is nothing sadder than giving time, energy, money, and love to complete a book, only to see it collect dust instead of sales. As much, or more, time must be allocated to marketing as to your writing.

My marketing includes a multi-pronged approach consisting of:

- **Building an email list**—communicating directly with prospective and happy readers is key to any authors' success. The number one way a reader learns about a book is from another reader. Your email list is the best way to build relationships with your readers and turn them into super fans who share your books with others.

A subscriber list can be tremendously powerful, but it takes time to build. Starting even before the book is released can have a HUGE impact in the long run. It will also help you begin connecting with the individuals that will become your readers.

In addition, subscriber lists can grow to be incredibly complex, meaning there is a learning curve that will take time to master. Learning it all at once when you are writing full-time can have a detrimental impact on your career because of the drain on your time. Writing like a boss is about being smart, and planning ahead is *very* smart.

- **Social Media**—while I'm not entirely sure new readers find books to read by seeing them posted *by me* on social media, nevertheless I know social media is an important part of my book marketing strategy because I can connect and interact with my readers, fans, and super fans. I even have a fun hashtag, #cultofHonoree, given to me and started on Instagram by a fan.

Social Media is essential in today's market, and creating your presence early can help you connect with those interested in your content. As you prepare your content for publication you can test covers and blurbs, measuring the responses so you can publish a final book that stands out. This very act tends to excite your fledgling readership, causing it to expand as they like and share news of your upcoming release.

Pro Tip: Don't make the effort to utilize every social media platform. Doing so can be both daunting and counterproductive. Having a presence on each site is good, but a better strategy is to target your attention to a few sites, and draw your readers there.

- **Amazon Marketing Ads and Facebook Advertising.** I defer to my author buddy, Brian Meeks, and of course Ben when it comes to ads (I know enough to be dangerous). Advertising is an important part of any writer's marketing strategy and there are plenty of resources available to help you learn what you need to know.

  Advertising on Amazon and Facebook may not begin early, but a clear understanding of these elements will help you know when to start. Publishing has a window of opportunity where advertising is most effective. If you want to *Write Like a Boss* you must **Learn Like a Boss!** And that starts before you publish. I consider writing to be just fifty percent of my job, with editing, marketing, and publishing filling in the rest. Learning the marketing and business while you write will give you a big step up when you publish.

- **Networking with other writers and authors.** And this, my friends, is how we find ourselves here.

Through the miracle of writer's conferences, I met the incredible Ben Hale, we formed a friendship based on mutual respect (and in my case, true admiration). Writing can be a lonely gig (perfect for introverts like me), but there's no one else that can understand the trials, tribulations, and nuances, help you strategize, and offer words of encouragement like another writer! It is important to find other folks who are at your same level— so you can grow together. And, you'll want to find someone who has been in the game longer so you can learn from them (and avoid costly mistakes).

Networking is an intangible idea that can be difficult to make tangible. Meeting other authors undoubtedly makes a big impact, forging friendships that will shape your career and support you in times of trial. But how do we quantify it? We make it tangible. My first book conference was at Indie Book Fest in Orlando. I spent about $500 between the table, the books, travel, etc. I sold two books and made $4 after the cost of the books. When I got home, I was a touch discouraged.

Here's what I did. I took a piece of paper and made three columns. In column one I put the names of those I'd met, and in column two I put the ideas I'd learned from them. But it's the third column that gets interesting, because I wrote down the **VALUE of the Ideas**. For advertising tips, I estimated a value over five years, for writing ideas I estimated ten. To my shock, the value of the event topped $100,000!

Seriously! Networking can have a MASSIVE impact on your career, so start while you are still writing!

We want to stay on track here, so in *Market Like a Boss,* we'll cover both of our marketing plans and schedules in depth. Suffice it to say each of the four marketing strategies above are necessary for your success and must find a regular place on your calendar.

Finally, the **rest of your life.** In my mind, my writing business serves the purpose of supporting my life and lifestyle. I truly, genuinely, deeply *love writing*, and yet it is not my raison d'être. My reason for being is deeper than that and includes exploring the world, spending time and creating magic moments with my family, as well as writing for entertainment and inspirational purposes.

There are times in any professional writer's life when an increased word count is important to meet a deadline. In fact, every professional's day-to-day schedule has peaks and valleys of pressure to perform. To be a productive and creative writer, however, there must be time when there is no writing.

No writing, you say?

Yes, yes, I did. If every single moment of every single day is scheduled to the hilt with activities, there is no time to rest, relax, and recharge.

Honorée, you are a wonder. I had not even thought about including this principle in this book, but it is essential to writing like a boss. Like anything else, doing too much can burn you out. You need to push yourself, but not to the breaking point. If I had tried to hit my current goals in my first year, I would have felt like bread in a toaster set on **"10."** (Don't try it!) Writing requires energy and time, and pushing yourself too hard too quickly can have a detrimental effect on your career. I've seen authors overcommit themselves so much that their creative process is destroyed, and their career plummets. Be relentless, but don't break yourself!

Rest

My book business action plan includes time off for days off, short and long vacations, three-day weekends, and several naps during the week. I define rest as *doing nothing* or *doing as little as possible.* Sleeping in, slowing down my pace, spending time alone or with my family and friends all qualify.

Relax

Take a deep breath, exhale, and feel your shoulders drop. You just relaxed—now grab a book with a great story, brew a cup of tea, cover yourself with a cozy blanket and let the story take you away. Doesn't that sound terrific? We all need time to do activities that simply aren't work.

Recharge

Finally, I recommend recharging via meditation or other mindfulness activities. Another way to recharge is "courting the muse," where one is in pursuit of inspiration through television and film, museums, galleries or other art, or the grandest inspiration herself: Mother Nature. Every night I put my phone on the charger because I work that gal hard every day. As humans, we also need to disconnect from the hectic pace of productivity and plug into whatever we need to recharge our own batteries.

I won't spend a ton of time on meditation, but it deserves a solid mention! This is one of my ninja tricks for producing so much, so quickly. I meditate every day and I crave that time when my mind can shut off completely and "reboot." Just as we must turn off our computer completely on a regular basis so it may reboot correctly, our minds must be given the opportunity to shut down and reboot. If you haven't discovered just how incredible meditation can be, give it a try and see for yourself. Grab the app Headspace and do ten minutes for ten days. I know from experience you will find yourself less stressed and more creative—just for starters.

I also do a longer meditation when I don't get enough sleep (hi, I'm a mom, it happens all the time!), and that gets me through the day without any casualties (smile). It doesn't matter that I was awake last night for an entire hour (thank you, Mr. Sylvester Pickles, my tuxedo kitty), I still needed to get up and write the words in this book to stay on schedule.

One last thing about meditation: it doesn't take time away from you (in case you're thinking: *I don't have time to do what needs doing, let alone finding time to literally sit and do nothing!*), it actually gives you time. You will find you are more productive, get things done in less time, and are more creative and inspired than ever before—

with a simple meditation practice. What have you got to lose? (Answer: not a thing!)

Go too long without rest, relaxation, or a good recharge and you'll find yourself squarely in burn-out. You run the risk of losing your drive to write (oh no!) or worse, face the idea you might not want to be a writer at all.

A few years ago, I wrote an entire 70,000-word nonfiction book in eight days. I was also going through a tough time personally. I forged ahead each day with my stress levels at an unbearable level. Once I turned in the manuscript, I got very sick. Double-Z-Pak-in-bed-for-days sick-as-a-dog sick. *Not good.* I didn't have anything left to give anyone, especially the person who needed me most. It was awful!

It is tempting to press forward, to work *all the time*, produce more, get more done, and speak of a time later "after I'm successful" when time off will be enjoyed. Please don't do that yourself. Don't do that to your health, or your family, or friends.

A truly successful writer is a writer who enjoys, yes, truly loves writing. And they also enjoy other activities and allow themselves the soul-nourishing time to do nothing at all. Trust me when I say you will be a happier, more productive, more prosperous writer when you add rest, relaxation, and time to recharge to your full-time writer action plan.

I love writing, but I live for family. With six kids and an incredible wife, I work so I can spend time with them. I've talked about how I block my time earlier in this book.

In case you have forgotten, I block out five weeks of personal time each year that I use for holidays, Christmas time and anything else my family needs. But that doesn't solve the problem of how to manage the daily workload.

But let's start with a question. Why do you write? Do you want to travel? Learn new things? Visit castles? Meet new people? Or just stay at home in your pajamas? (You know who you are!) We love to write but we hope for more from our writing. I write so I can have time with my family, therefore my goals are centered around creating time. For example, on a given day I'll set a goal to write faster so I can get off and see my kids when they get home from school. Or I might set a goal to write extra so I can get a day off on Friday for a weekend trip with my family. These times recharge me and excite me, so it becomes a cycle of motivation.

I set goals that **push me**.

I set goals that **excite me.**

You want to write like a boss? Set goals that excite and empower you, goals that drag you out of bed before dawn, goals that keep you up at night. You don't just want to write, you want to live, and your goals reflect that. Set a goal to go out to dinner when you write 3,000 words in a day, and a goal to visit Hawaii when you reach 100,000 sales. Resting and recharging are part of your plan because being a writer is more than just typing, it's a way of life.

I get ideas when I rest, when I vacation, when I travel, when I'm with my family and my friends. As you make writing a way of life you'll discover that inspiration is *everywhere*. Take notes! On your phone or on paper, take notes when you have ideas.

As you rest and relax you'll find your mind filling up with new ideas and inspiration. You'll need this to recharge your creative batteries because when you write you'll burn them to a crisp, and then recharge them again. Writing Like a Boss isn't just writing, it's **becoming a writer**.

We've covered the main aspects of your writing business. You know what needs to be done: create **Your Full-Time Writer Action Plan.** When that's ready, you'll want to ...

3

JUST DO IT

When my alarm sounds at 5:30 a.m., my personal rule dictates that I just get up. No internal argument (but it's warm in bed and cold out there!), no snooze button (what is an extra nine minutes going to do anyway?), no delay. I just get up and get moving. (I'm terrible at this, so I have huge respect for Honorée!)

How do I do it? Well, I just do it! Easier said than done, without question, "just do it" works when paired with other initiatives. If it were just that easy, everyone would do it and the planet would be chock full of productive, happy writers, cranking out thousands of words without a mention of the cursed writer's block.

Wait, Do YOU Believe in Writer's Block?

That is perhaps my favorite question when listening to Kelton Reid talk to successful writers on his podcast *The Writer Files*. Although there are two schools of thought, those who believe writer's block exists and those who don't, it is interesting to me that ninety percent (give or take) of his guests do not believe in writer's block at all.

Most writers, including famous ones, struggle with it from time to time. There is nothing more terrifying and frustrating to a writer than to sit down at the keyboard only to have no words appear on the screen. Some writers suffer for weeks or months, others have tried to break free from the block by using drugs or alcohol. Just a little block can cause someone to become unsure of themselves and quit altogether.

But I question the validity of it, still, because I think of it this way: why isn't there a block for any profession? You can't have lawyer's block, secretary's block, or housekeeper's block—i.e., *I'm just not feeling it today, I can't draft that contract, answer the phone, or clean that shower today.*

I'm firmly planted in the "writer's block doesn't exist" camp. Here's why: I believe when I sit down to write, the words flow easily from my fingertips.

I learned this from listening to Dan Kennedy's *The New Psycho-Cybernetics* audio program, based on Dr. Maxwell Maltz's original program (which I highly recommend). Dan must produce the equivalent word count of two full-sized novels each month. When he said,

When I sit down to write, I don't have the luxury of not writing. When I sit down to write, I write. I thought to myself, "That's a great belief. I'm going to go with that!" Funnily enough, that was *years* before I decided to write my first blog post, let alone my first book. I didn't know it at the time, but that belief would come in mighty handy time and time again as I began to produce more and more books.

I agree with Honorée about writer's block—to a point. Even before I began writing full time I viewed writing as an occupation. When I set writing time, I had to write, and not writing wasn't an option. Because of this perspective, I wrote three books in three years, the trilogy that went on to sell 10,000 copies in the first six months.

For me, writing nonfiction is much easier to push past writer's block, because I'm merely gathering thoughts that already exist in my head. Writing about a topic I know is as simple as sitting and forcing the action. But fiction is a different game because I'm not writing what I know, I'm forging a story that doesn't exist.

Writer's block can be one of the best things you encounter as a writer. And once you understand its purpose, I think you'll agree. Writer's block is merely a tool, one of many you will learn to use to your advantage. I believe it exists, but more importantly, I know how to use it to **improve my writing**. In the next section I'll describe how.

How to Get Over It or Avoid It Altogether

You don't have to get stuck in writer's block. You can either elude it, or even foil it if you find yourself stuck in it.

There are two important things to remember when it comes to writer's block:

1. **There are ways to prevent it.** One is to not believe in it, the other is to develop a belief that counteracts it.

2. **There are ways to break through it.** You can figure out your trigger—more on this in an upcoming section—and find yourself back in the flow of creativity with some simple strategies.

You don't have to settle for blocks and the delays, frustrations, and other challenges they bring with them. I hope you've never had a block, but if you have, here's help you can use right now.

Develop Your Rock-Solid Belief

Just like your *I am* statement from Chapter 2, it is helpful to identify the best belief (the one that serves you) and just start believing it.

You can program your brain, through the adoption of a powerful belief that you, too, can write anytime you want! Imagine being able to sit down at your computer, within minutes of waking, getting on a plane, or even sitting in a hospital waiting room and instantly produce brand new words. With no warm-up, and no need to "get into the mood" you *can* pour words onto paper at a breakneck pace. Want to know more? I thought you would!

The only way to do this consistently, and without developing an ulcer or burnout, is to decide two things:

1. You can't afford *not* to write when it's time to write.

2. Whenever you sit down to write, the words pour effortlessly from your fingertips, regardless of what is happening around you.

As a professional writer, *writing like a boss* means you must consistently produce quality words on a constant basis. You can't afford the luxury of staring at your screen, cursor blinking unemotionally, while you wait for the words to come. Time, as they say, is money. In this case, your product is the accumulation of words, and words are money. I'll assume we can agree you don't have an hour or a day to waste.

In that case, you'll need to define the belief you want to install in your subconscious and get after it. You might like mine: *Every time I sit down to write, I easily and effortlessly write!*

Now just to be clear: I have days where I feel less-than-enthusiastic about that 4:30 a.m. wake-up alarm or my 5:53 a.m. alarm reminder that it's "almost time to write!" I am genuinely in love with writing; it is wonderful for my soul. And, let's face it, too much of something is sometimes just too much (which is why I reinforced the powers of rest, relaxation, and recharging so much in the previous chapter). I love iced sugar cookies and I could eat three huge ones in one sitting. But after I do that, I kinda don't want another sugar cookie (at least until tomorrow). The same with writing—when I do extra hours of writing on any given day, sometimes *I am over it* by the time I close the lid on my laptop.

I access my belief, and remind myself of it, anytime its needed. You'll want to do the same. Before you continue, identify your new belief. (It's okay, I'll wait right here.)

Do THIS When You Find Yourself Blocked

So that shiny new belief you just crafted? Yeah, you might be wondering how exactly you're going to adopt it as gospel, when up to this point you've been struggling. I recommend a two-pronged approach, so simple and easy you're either not going to want to do it, or you're going to think it won't work.

Look, I'm an expert at uninstalling crappy beliefs and installing the ones that make me look like I'm super-human (my clients call me Batman for a reason). So, if you'll indulge me, you just might find yourself writing more than you ever thought possible in a very short time. Isn't it worth it to hear me out? Okay, good.

Idea Number One: Write your belief fifteen times in one sitting, every single day. I won't extol the virtues of affirmations here, just trust me on this one, okay? Get a notebook or use your journal, and write that sucker down. Over and over and over.

Idea Number Two: Say your new belief over and over, hundreds or even thousands of times per day. Use something to remind you to do it, like locking or unlocking a door, going to the bathroom, or hearing the phone ring. You can say it silently to yourself while brushing your teeth, while you're making an eight-pump chai for your regular customer at your Starbucks barista gig, or even out loud while you shower or drive to work.

Why do these triggers work so well? The repetition eventually overrides whatever belief you currently have. It works so well that eventually you'll just find yourself doing whatever you've been telling yourself you wanted to do. Literally, in the middle of a three-thousand-word sprint, you'll stop and say, "Holy cow! I really *am* a writer who easily writes three thousand words a day! Whoa!" Just like with me, it will probably sneak up on you, and it will be a mighty nice surprise when it does.

Figure Out Your Trigger

You are probably a writing lover like me, which is why you even had the idea of *writing like a boss* in the first place! And on those days when you don't feel like leaping out of bed, chock full of ideas, with the urge to write like a champion, there are several things I've discovered that put me in the writing state. I'll share mine with you, and hopefully they will spawn some new ones for you.

First, let me explain what I mean by *figure out your trigger*. There are certain triggers that cause us to feel like doing something (or like doing nothing). When I hear the final score of *Rocky* begin, I feel like I could run another mile, faster than the one I just finished. When I hear anything by Enya, I'm instantly depressed. I'm sure you could list off a few things that raise you up or pull you down.

One of my principal triggers is situational. I have a space that is my office, and when I am there I write. My current home has an office, but my old house didn't have the room. I wrote in a corner of my master bedroom, literally three feet of space. This presented a whole host of problems.

I had three children at the time and they LOVED to come in and climb into my lap. "Daddy hug?" they would say, and how could I deny them? This was the best type of distraction. But it was still a distraction. If that wasn't enough, I would occasionally hear my kids crying in the other room and, as a father, want to help. Other times my incredible wife would come in and all my attention would turn to her, because she is captivating.

So how was I supposed to write? When I was in that seat, I was not at home. I created a trigger when I sat in that chair and it was strong enough to carry me through three years of writing. My wife would call my phone even though she was in the next room—sometimes from inside the room. If I didn't pick up, she accepted that I couldn't and gave me the support I needed to write. (This is the moment I confirm that my wife deserves much of the credit for my work!) That trigger was the foundation of my career. Identify your triggers and learn to use them.

You can imagine, then, it would be a mighty fine idea to pinpoint what really makes you feel like writing, despite anything that might be blocking your path. Identifying your writing triggers will make a huge difference in whether you feel like writing—or not. Another cool tool you can use is the practice of rituals.

Ben also makes a great point about getting the support you need from your spouse or significant other. As I write this sentence, my daughter is in her room and my husband is on the couch working. I'm hiding out in our room, reviewing this book and adding the finishing touches. Without their support, I simply wouldn't be able to get my writing done.

Have the conversations you need to have, set the boundaries you need to set, and you will be able to get your writing done.

Use the Power of Rituals

You brush your teeth every night before bed, a ritual that started as a habit (which began when you were a small child, usually followed by story time and bedtime). You probably don't even think about this nightly ritual; you just do it like clockwork. The result is a whiter smile, no cavities or gum disease, and (my favorite) less trips to the dentist. In its own way, this simple daily ritual is perpetually transformative.

As aspiring writers in a world dominated by Facebook, a 24-hour news cycle, and a constant demand to cross items off our to-do lists, it may seem difficult to develop new rituals.

One of the best ways to unlock your inner power is to create a new daily ritual, and it is best to start small when doing so. Through the ancient teachings of yoga, we know that our thoughts lead to actions; our actions become habits; our habits form our character; and our character determines our destiny. Instituting a new daily ritual is the act of taking your newly-adopted *I am* statements and putting them into action using a ritual. You are what you think, and once a positive ritual takes hold in your life, you don't even need to think about it anymore. Just like you brush your teeth, so shall you "just write your words—it will just happen."

Here are five simple steps to help you adopt your new ritual:

Set Your Intention

Close your eyes and ask yourself, "What habit would most serve me in my writing career right now?" The answer, which just might be your new belief statement, is your intention.

Habits are tricky things, especially in writing. An intention rarely turns into actions, and even more rarely does it turn into a habit. When Honorée asks, "What habit would most serve me in my writing career," the focus you should find is the word "habit", not "intention". Let's take it from the beginning.

Intention is thought.

A thought turns into action.

An action turns into frequent action.

Frequent action turns into habit.

Habit turns into multiple habits.

Multiple habits turn into a career.

Knowing the steps means you can follow them. I began where everyone does, with the intention to write a book. I began with an action, write one chapter. This action led to other actions, to writing more chapters. Over time this became a frequent action, of writing three times a week, and then four, and finally five. As my discipline grew so did my skill, until I crossed the invisible threshold and writing became a habit. This entire process took about two years for me, and during the next two I added other habits. I began research and marketing, editing and connecting with other authors. I invested *four years* into my growing passion before it launched my fledgling career.

The point is, you can program yourself to build a career. Look at the above list and figure out where you are. If you are writing occasionally, congrats, you are at stage two. The trick is that it requires intention to push past each stage. You can get stuck at the writing occasionally stage forever if you don't decide you want more. It may sound simple, but it's hard to put into practice. As I said, it took me four years. Others take more, and I've met some that took less. Regardless, use this as a map to elevate intentions to habits.

Start Small

Rome wasn't built in a day, and going from a couple of hundred words to multi-thousand-word writing days won't happen overnight. A great question is: "What is one small, doable step I can take in the direction of my intention?" Rather than trying to make massive changes in your writing life all at once (and set yourself up for disappointment), use small victories to build your confidence instead. Guess what? These will soon lead to bigger victories. (Duh!)

Channel Your Inner Writer Hero

Name a writer who is just crushing it, and channel them. Ben has inspired me to take my writing game up a few notches. Make your writing inspiration your alter ego and ask yourself, *What would they do?* I happen to know Ben writes 3,500 words a day, so when I'm "not feeling it," I know he *is*, and I choose what I think he'd do instead of what I feel like doing (Netflix binge watching, anyone?). Channeling and visualizing your writing hero consistently every time you need a boost will eventually mean you'll be your own hero.

When channeling your inner hero, make sure you remember that they started where you are. A great example can inspire you, but don't let it discourage you. Your writer hero shows you that the path has been conquered, that you can follow in their footsteps. But the journey is still your own. Lean on their example when you need confidence, and in time you will find your own.

Ben, you make a terrific point! I wasn't always able to write like a boss, it took time and graduating from one level to the next to really find my groove. Hold yourself accountable, dream big, and don't beat yourself up when you don't succeed the first (or fortieth) time.

Honor the Ritual

While you brush your teeth every morning, remind yourself of your intention. Take your small steps in the direction of your intention with confidence and conviction. Reaffirm the positive habit you are adopting every day until suddenly you notice it has become second nature.

Release the Outcome

We live in a microwave popcorn and instant coffee society, teaching us to expect quick, effortless change. True transformation takes time, I'm happy to report. And remember, the longer it takes the more permanent it is. Release your need for instant gratification and, in its place, honor your ritual. You know in your heart your new ritual (and the results it will ultimately bring) is good for you. The outcome you desire will come to pass and when it does, you will be ready!

Keep in mind you created the positive habit of daily brushing even though you hated it as a kid (why else would your mom have to remind you for the first few months?!).

I have to remind my kids daily to brush their teeth. And by daily, I mean six or seven times for each brushing. I am creating the ritual in my children by repeating it twenty times a day. But it's a lifetime habit I'm attempting to create, so it's worth the repetition.

Here are a few of my rituals, you might consider using them as an example or as a basis for your own:

Morning—I have a morning ritual that includes getting dressed for the gym, drinking a large glass of water, and pouring myself a cup of coffee. This ritual in and of itself signals me that it's time to write. Before I start writing, I check my sales dashboards and see if there are any new reviews for my books from the day before (it's encouraging to see that people are buying and enjoying my books). Then, at the stroke of 6 a.m., I open my WIP, search for "H is here" (where I left off from the previous writing session), and start writing.

A consistent morning ritual will seep into your subconscious over time and it will become a habit to write at that time.

Music—Music is a huge trigger for me! There are certain songs that engage my writing muscles and get them firing like nothing else I've found.

Movies—I'm inspired by movies such as *Rudy, Rocky* (especially *Rocky II*), and *Moneyball*. I have them saved on my DVR and when I need some motivation I watch one. We find ourselves in other people's stories, and I am always inspired by watching them (even though I've seen them a zillion times). I also believe laughter *is* the best medicine, so I love comedies like *Hitch, When Harry Met Sally,* and *Airplane.*

Music and movies are just two examples of ways to get in an inspired state which can lead to writing—the side bonus is they both allow a combination of rest and relaxation to occur while "doing" them. It's up to you to figure out what works best for you and throw it on your schedule.

Evening—I engage in an evening ritual as well; I call it my "Power Down" ritual. After I throw on some pajamas, do a few minutes of yoga, read my Quiet Time Ritual (a.k.a., QTR, from *The Power of Consistency* by Weldon Long), and then take in some fiction. This signifies to my mind, body, and spirit it is time to go to sleep.

Studies show our first thoughts in the morning are often the last thought we had as we drifted off to sleep. In *The Power of Positive Thinking,* Dr. Norman Vincent Peale talks about how our minds really pay attention to the last thoughts we have. In my QTR, I reinforce my beliefs that when it's time to write, I'm raring and ready to *write like a boss.*

Some of you may be thinking this is pointless, that it's theory that will never amount to anything. But Honorée and I have applied these principles to improve our lives and forge the careers we love. These are self-hacks, and they can change the fabric of what you believe about yourself.

Writing like a boss isn't like a normal career. A normal job requires you to work, even giving you task lists to accomplish. You probably work for someone who has their own lists and tasks, all laid out for them by someone higher up.

To be a writer you must organize your life in such a manner to master yourself. You aren't just the writer, *you are the boss*. And that's what this boils down to. Most individuals lack the discipline to motivate themselves, so they require an employer to keep them motivated. If you want to write like a boss you must **become the boss**.

All these things–triggers, habits, inner heroes–are all intended to help you learn how shed the doubt and fear that all writers begin with. Some of our comments may help you a great deal, others not so much. That's okay. What's important for us is that you begin to see a roadmap to reaching your dreams. Too often we imagine a dream but it seems so far out of reach that we can never attain it, so we make the gravest mistake of all, we don't try.

As I write these words it's 1:30 a.m. and I have to get up at 7:00. But my boss (me) is saying I need to stay late. I not only reached my word count today, but surpassed it. But my boss (still me) is relentless, constantly driving me to be better, to accomplish more. The reason I'm working late is because I want to go swimming with my kids tomorrow afternoon. I want to take time off, so boss (yep, still me) said that if I hit 5,000 words for the day, I can take half the day off tomorrow.

Now, I obviously don't have an actual voice in my head telling me I have to work late. What I do have is the knowledge that if I want to go swimming with my kids tomorrow, I still have to finish the work by tomorrow night. Which means a late night today. Let's lay this out.

- I have a vision of time with my family.

- I have a goal to teach my third child how to swim.

- I have a goal to hit an average writing count of 3,500 words.

- I know I can do it because I've done it before.

- So, I do it. (And he does it like a boss!)

In short, I'm applying the principles I'm writing about *on the same day I'm writing it.* I am a full-time writer because I have developed the personal habits and skills to be the boss as well as the writer.

For the record, my boss isn't so bad. He doesn't provide dental, but hey, you can't beat the hours. Plus, I get to choose my co-workers. And Honorée is the best kind. (Awww, shucks!)

You will want to identify your writing triggers, and engage in them on a regular basis. I think there's nothing more of a bummer than having a slice of time to write and not being able to crank out the words. Figure out what makes you tick, what gets your juices flowing, and make a list while those ideas are fresh in your mind. The next time you're at a loss for what to do, crack open your list and pick one of them to do.

I know if you use the information provided in this chapter you will begin to write like a boss before you know it. When you're ready, choose to read Ben's Chapter: The Fiction Boss, or my Chapter: The Nonfiction Boss, to find out how to write your next book *like a boss!*

4

THE FICTION BOSS

love to write fiction. As of this writing I have written and published seventeen books that all connect into a massive world and timeline. By the end of this year it will be nineteen, with more fiction planned in the next few years. If I keep the same pace, I'll have forty books by the time I'm forty years old.

So far, we've talked a lot about motivation, goals, and vision. While it is essential to your efforts, it doesn't help you become a better writer. In this chapter, we're going to talk about the actual work of writing, how to improve sentence structure, vocabulary, and overall style. Creative writing is a talent that requires dedication, learning, and discipline to master.

Everyone has their own style, what we call our voice. You might think your author's voice is an innate aspect of your personality, and to a certain degree that is true. What you can change is the *clarity* of your voice. Let's use an example.

My daughter is ten and loves to write. She's already written the first few chapters of her first book. (I know, proud daddy moment.) When I read it, I notice the hallmarks of her fledgling voice, but that voice is obscured by several things, such as poor grammar, limited vocabulary, and lack of an overall knowledge of writing.

Throughout this section of the book I encourage you to take notes of the things you can change. You'll find multiple ways to clarify your author voice so it can connect to your target readers.

Do not be afraid to learn because that's exactly what's required for you to reach the vision you marked in the first chapter. This section is by no means an exhaustive analysis of creative writing, (that would be thousands of pages and rather tedious, I suspect) but rather a foundation for the most impactful elements I've discovered. So, let's get started with the basics, are you a pantser or a plotter?

What's Your Writing Style?

Pantser—You write by the seat of your pants (hence the name). You have no idea where the story is going because it drives itself. A character dies and you are just as upset as a reader.

Greatest advantage: Creativity flows easier for you, and you just need the discipline to turn it on. Once you do, the sky's the limit.

Greatest disadvantage: You don't know where the story is going so you can't plan ahead. It will always be harder to make your stories seamless because each sequel can feel like an appendage rather than a part of a grand whole.

How to compensate: Trust your instincts. Keep writing and let the story flow where it wants to go. Some of the best stories are written by pantsers.

Plotter—You have to visualize where you want to go, and once you do it's like a favorite movie. Then you write with passion, creating a story both complex and exciting.

Greatest advantage: Creativity flows easily once you imagine it, and your story can be far more intricate. Design big and write big; your stories will reflect that.

Greatest disadvantage: You have difficulty writing unless you have a clear idea of the chapter, scene, and story. This can cause you to sit and stare at the screen, shackled by indecision.

How to compensate: For you, much of story creation occurs in the planning. Recognize it. Own it. Write ideas down whenever they come, so by the time you are ready to write you will know where you want to go. Also, keep in mind that the flow of ideas *can* be increased, so push that ability until it flows easily.

Don't be something you're not. Regardless of whether you are a pantser or plotter, keep in mind that these are not opposites, they fit together along a gradient. Most plotters will follow an unexpected plot in the moment, and every pantser knows some of the future. Identify where you are at on the spectrum and how to maximize your placement.

10 Rules to a Bestselling Story

Regardless of your writing style, crafting a story is always a challenge. But I want to pass on a few ideas that should help you take your story to the next level, and I've put them into rules.

Rule # 10 - **Vary your language**. Repetitive content is boring, especially if you use the same words throughout the book. When I started writing I was shocked to learn my vocabulary was terrible. I set out to learn new words, and I'm still learning.

Rule # 9 – **Vary your sentence structure**. If every sentence starts with He/She, your story is going to feel very static. Punch it up by changing the structure. I won't go into an exhaustive example, but if you need help on this one, google it. You'll find tons of examples.

Rule # 8 – **Vary your sentence length**. I did an analysis of Harry Potter once and found that the sentences vary from just eight words all the way to almost forty—in the same paragraph. Variability in your sentence length creates a sense of excitement that really punches up your book.

Rule # 7 – **End word focus**. People naturally remember more from the end of a sentence, chapter, book etc. Ending on a preposition, such as 'it,' is weak and not as memorable. Always try to end on a noun or verb. Better yet, use a strong noun or verb.

Rule # 6 – **Detail vs Pacing**. The more detail you have the slower the book, the less detail, the faster. The *Lord of the Rings* is a mainstay of fantasy fiction, and it's incredibly detailed. Know which you are.

Rule # 5 – **Know your writer's crutch**. Every writer has at least one. It could be overusing certain words, or it could be the story gets weak in the middle. Learn to recognize your crutches and then avoid them.

Rule # 4 – **Parallel Language**. This is a big one, and is especially useful in book descriptions. Here's an example many know from history. "I came to bury Caesar, not to praise him." Parallel language is when the sentence mirrors itself in a creative and clever way. Most importantly, it's memorable. But be careful not to overuse it. Think of parallel language like spice. A little will delight. A lot will destroy. (See the parallel?)

Rule # 3 - **Adverbs/Adjectives**. You will occasionally hear authors say never use them, but I would say use them cautiously. (See the adverb there?) Adverbs modify verbs and adjectives modify nouns, both add to your text and usually make your content wordy and excessive. Try to use a stronger noun/verb and lose the adjective/ adverb. Quick tip, search your manuscript for LY. Most adverbs have -ly at the end, and you may be shocked by how many you use. Delete as many as you can and tighten that language!

Rule # 2 – Never stop learning. Writing is a journey that requires discipline and courage, and the unyielding dedication to grow. Master *every* aspect of writing and publishing and your chances of attaining your vision will skyrocket. Today's publishing world is fluid and dynamic, constantly changing to adapt to new markets, new marketing tools, and new opportunities. To become successful, you must get used to learning, and never stop. Complacency can kill your vision as quickly as doubt.

Rule # 1 – What's the first rule of writing strong fiction? **Editing**. There is just as much creation in editing as there is in writing. Don't make the mistake of thinking your first draft is high quality. My draft process is thirteen drafts. But it didn't start out that way. My first book went through twenty-four drafts and still has errors. Figure out a draft process that works for you and then stick to it until it becomes routine. (I'll go over my 13 drafts in a moment.)

These ten rules may be daunting, but tackle them with commitment and focus and one day you will master them all. Creative writing is a talent like any other and comes down to refining your author voice until it's dynamic, exciting, intriguing, and memorable. Until it goes from a whisper to a roar.

Remember, writing is a medium to evoke emotion. If you want to be a powerful author, learn to evoke emotion and you'll be stunned by what you write.

Editing

Editing deserves its own category, and there's a lot that needs to be addressed here. Like I mentioned before, there is just as much creation in editing as there is in writing. That's because on the second, third, or seventh read-through you will have new ideas in *response to your own work*. This can take your book in an entirely new direction, or just tighten a single paragraph. A specific draft process will help you refine a book. I'll share mine here, but keep in mind that you don't have to follow my process. You can and should use it as a template, but feel free to add your own drafts or subtract until you have a system that works for you.

Pro tip: Record how long it takes you to do each draft. Then, add up the days so you know how long it takes you to edit a book. It will help you make and keep goals.

Ben Hale's Draft Process

Draft 0 – Outline. Yes, there's a draft Zero. This is the outline for me. I start big and go small. I'll outline the series, then the books, then the sections, and then the chapters. Only then do I start writing. Now I don't have to go into that much detail, but the more I know, the faster I write.

Draft 1 – Finish. This draft is all about finishing. I want to get to THE END. I'll skip a section if I don't know it and keep writing, but the goal here is to get done with the story. My average first draft is 85k-90k words.

Draft 2 – Content. Here I am trying to fill in holes, expand content, add detail, etc., and generally flesh out the book until it feels complete.

Draft 3 – Alpha reader. Alpha readers review a book early in the draft process to give feedback on the whole content. They are harder to find than beta readers and must possess the ability to look past typos, glaring omissions, and grammatical problems. A good one will look at your story and help you know what's missing, and what's working.

Draft 4 – Character building. Here I focus on characters and comments from the alpha reader, adding detail to the characters to make them more three dimensional and "real."

Draft 5 – Editor. The all-important editor draft. Building a relationship with an editor is essential to your craft. Need help finding one? They tend to frequent places where you find other authors. Ask other authors and you'll find an editor in no time.

Draft 6 – Post Editor Partial. When I get my book back from my editor (she's incredible, by the way), I go through and accept or reject her comments. For the most part I accept any spelling/grammatical things but with story elements I may not. More complicated ones I leave for the Post Editor Full. I do NOT read the whole book on this draft.

Draft 7 – Post Editor Full. Now that the book is free of red ink, I focus on the story with the editor's comments in mind. If she said the ending is weak I'll focus on that, or if a certain chapter seems unnecessary, etc.

Draft 8 – Word Draft. Throughout my editing process I make notes on various things to find and replace. Cap this character's name, double check I didn't use this name in another book, search for adverbs, etc. I also use spell check here. This gets it ready for the beta readers.

Draft 9 – Beta Readers. These special readers read a book in advance of publication and help me refine the book. They catch anything from typos to continuity errors, and really help tighten the overall book. I've changed entire endings because of them, and my books are better for it. Pro tip: Have at least five, and they all have to be honest.

Draft 10 – Post Beta Reader Partial. Here I'll do the same thing I did with my editor, and just go through and make changes based on what my editor suggested.

Draft 11 – Vocal Draft. I've found this to be one of the best drafts I use, because reading it out loud gets me to catch things that are easy to otherwise miss. Doing this draft at the end really helps fine tune the book and prepare it for publication.

Draft 12 – Final Beta Reader. Not everyone does this, but I like to have a final beta reader go through my book after I've done the vocal draft. Sometimes I create a stupid typo and they help me catch it. Or, they just find things missed by everyone else.

Draft 13 – Final and Format. After getting it back from my final beta reader I'll go through their comments, which are hopefully just typos and other small changes. Once that's done I begin the format process which includes chapter headings, front matter, and back matter.

You're done!

Like I said, this draft process is not for everyone. In fact, it probably only works for me. But hopefully it helps you get a start on your own if you don't already have one. Don't be afraid to add entire drafts as you learn how to refine your writer's voice. Also, keep in mind that with more practice, your draft process will shrink.

Writer's Block

No section on creative writing would be complete without talking about writer's block. Honorée has done an excellent analysis of writer's block in an earlier chapter, but I want to cover it from a fiction angle.

I do believe writer's block exists, but I don't believe it has to block you. Writer's block affects every fiction writer, young and old, new and experienced, amateur and professional. It stops our creativity and slows our writing down, sometimes for days, weeks, or even years at a time. Since it's an experience we all share, let's talk about how it can be conquered.

The first thing to understand about writer's block is that it can come from a lack of ideas. I've found that ideas come from EVERYWHERE. I've had ideas while doing laundry, building a treehouse, fixing a fence, playing soccer, snowboarding, vacuuming, hugging my son, waving to the mailman, etc. The important thing is to *write these ideas down*. Unless you have a perfect memory—which I certainly don't—then you need to take note of the ideas when they come. It takes practice to come up with ideas on the spot, but having a bank of ideas stored up makes it that much easier when it's time to write.

The previous section aside, trying to write when you are uninspired may indicate you need to write something else. When I was writing the third book of my *Master Thief Series*, I got stuck at a part and couldn't move past it. What did I do? I skipped it, all six chapters, and kept writing. I knew what I wanted there but couldn't seem to imagine it. I finished draft two and still couldn't figure it out. I gave the book to my alpha reader without a critical section! With her comments, I had an idea and ended up filling in entire section in just two days, six thousand words each day.

The third reason you might be struggling with writer's block is fairly simple: you know where you want the story to go but it won't go there. The solution to this particular problem is actually simple. The story is telling you it doesn't want to go in that direction, so listen! The more experienced you are the more you begin to see how a story drives itself, and the more you trust your voice, the better the story becomes.

These examples come to a simple conclusion—writer's block is a *good thing*! It pushes you to go in a different direction, get new ideas, or bring a new twist to the story. My most recent book (*The Rogue Mage*) had a section of basic training for the protagonist, but it felt very mundane. I wrestled with it for a while until I realized that the setting required a new training for mages that would incorporate magic. I created the Requiem, a sort of virtual reality where the characters could train inside the memory of other soldiers. The entire idea came because

I had writer's block. When you encounter it, don't try to break through, use it as a guide to find the greatness that lies beyond.

Know Your Genre

Most might consider world-building to be exclusive to fantasy or science fiction, but regardless of the genre you write in, you are creating a world. Your characters are unique, as are their relationships. Who are they related to? What are their character traits and flaws? Do they live in a fictional town or perhaps a fictional house? It doesn't matter if you are building a love story, a children's story, or an entire universe, you create worlds!

Creating these worlds means you need to know the **rules of your genre**. I'm not saying you can't bend or even break them, but you must know the rules to manipulate them. Just knowing the general rules for a genre will shape your writing, and help you connect with readers that are expecting certain aspects in your book. I could go into an exhaustive essay on the various genres and their rules but, frankly, I know very little of the rules in genres I don't write.

A basic example of a genre rule is the "happily ever after" in romance. Readers expect the two main characters to come together, happily, in the end. If you break this rule, you will end up with lots of unhappy readers (and perhaps one-star reviews)!

Writing about genre rules for each genre would be boring to anyone not writing in that genre. Suffice it to say, even a token effort at research will yield clear results on the elements of your genre. Even if you think you know it, don't skip this step!

A warning about world-building.

An often-repeated mistake in fantasy, and to a certain degree other genres, is the tendency to load world details on the front of the story. Remember Rule #6: Detail versus Pacing? If you take three chapters to describe the history of your story, the family connections, the relationships between characters and kingdoms, you've slowed the story down to a crawl. And readers will revolt. They will think the whole story is that way! Here are two good rules to follow to avoid this common mistake.

Rule #1: Don't provide history, backstory, descriptions (etc.), unless it is pertinent to the current event. Describe a forest as the character enters? Good. Describe the lineage of kings before meeting the prince, coming to the city, or otherwise going anywhere near the castle? Bad.

Rule #2: Trust the reader. Readers are adept at piecing together elements of a story. This applies even if the detail was read at the end of the book or the beginning, meaning they will come away with a complete idea even if you described a city four different ways throughout the book! The first time you may focus on the castle, the next time the waterfront (because you character is getting on a boat), the next time a secret entrance under the south tower, and the last time the thieves' guild hidden in a swamp outside the city. The reader will come away with a complete image even though you never described it in one sitting! This applies to a romance book as well, or a historical fantasy, or a paranormal action and adventure. Let the story organically reveal history or locations, and the book will be all the better.

Conversation

Conversation in writing was hard for me when I first began. As hard as I tried for the contrary, the statements seemed stilted and forced. The good news is that I didn't stop learning (remember Rule #2!), and my conversation got a lot better. Good conversation should stand on its own, and not need the speaking tags to describe them. Here's an example.

"I don't think we should do that," he grumbled.

Not too bad, but let's try to make it better.

"Do you want to get us killed?" he asked.

Do you notice the end word focus? (Rule # 7!) But let's try a step further.

He sneered at her suggestion. *"Do you want to get us killed?"*

Here we have a visual aspect, of his expression, and an end word focus in the dialogue. Much stronger. Conversation is much better when you sprinkle (Rule #10: Vary Your Language) visual things into the conversation. They show who is speaking while also illustrating tone and/or emotion. And when you think it's ready, read it out loud (Draft 11). If it's forced, you will probably hear it. If you are still unsure, ask a trusted beta reader to give you some feedback.

Passive vs. Active Voice

This is a simple element but it deserves its own section. In short, passive voice means things happen to the subject of a sentence.

Example: The story was written by Jane.

In this example Jane is almost irrelevant, an afterthought in her own story. Let's see the active version.

Example: Jane wrote a story.

In this example, Jane is the active participant, and the sentence feels stronger, more driven. You'll also notice the absence of *was*. Many writers have said that the verb *to be* is the weakest of the verbs, and I agree. Figuring out Passive vs. Active can be a challenge for even experienced writers, so don't feel bad if it's confusing. Just keep learning (Rule #2) and you'll master the active voice.

Doubt

Doubt is the worst aspect of being a writer. This insidious breaker of dreams threads its way into the minds of even great writers. It rises at the first bad review, the beta reader's comments, the editor's concerns, and even your spouse's worry. Writing is daunting enough without having to fight your doubt.

The good news is that doubt can be combated with courage. C. S. Lewis once said that, "Courage is not just one of the virtues, but the form of every virtue at the testing point."

The form of creativity at the testing point is writing, and the form of writing at the testing point is publishing. Both require courage, so the very act of **writing is an act of courage**.

I bet you didn't know that your hobby and soon-to-be-career requires courage! And just so you don't forget it, here are the Writing Laws of Courage

- **L - The Courage to Learn.** Remember Rule #2? Constantly learning is hard; it requires pushing yourself outside your comfort zone. Gather your courage and learn what you lack so you can become the great writer you know you can be.

- **A - The Courage to Adapt.** When life tries to stop you from writing, be relentless! Adapt to a new time, a new goal, a new vision. Have the courage to change and then keep writing!

- **W - The Courage to Write.** Have the courage to write when you are discouraged or happy, when your books are selling and when they're not. **Come what may—you write**.

- **S - The Courage to Soar.** When you attain your first vision it's easy to sit back and say, "I've made it." Don't. Have the courage to keep writing, to keep learning, to keep adapting. This career is rewarding, but don't wait until you are successful to be happy. Have the courage to be happy now.

The End

I hope you are now staring at several pages of notes that will help you clarify your writer's voice. Keep in mind that you don't have to tackle them all at once. Each of the principles take time to learn, practice, and master. If there are more than you expected, consider adding drafts to your draft process, each targeted at specific principles. You may do an entire draft just looking to tighten up vocabulary, or varying sentence structure. Remember the courage to Adapt!

I sincerely hope this section has helped you clarify your writer's voice. When I look at the early drafts of my first book, I cringe at the quality. But I'm also proud of my progress. When you are relentless in perfecting your craft, your voice goes from a whisper . . . to a roar.

5

THE NONFICTION BOSS

Much has been written about the design and craft of a nonfiction book. When I first started (when the Earth was still cooling), there weren't many resources I could consult. Back in the Dark Ages, self-publishing was *for losers*—at least that's what I heard. Here I am, getting the last laugh!

Anyway...

I did have some basic advice I used to get started, combined with some common sense. Mark Victor Hansen, in addition to telling me *"You must write a book,"* encouraged me to take my most popular speech, write it down, and turn it into a book.

My speech had been designed to give my audiences the most logical way to organize their life and double their success, and was titled similarly: *7 Master Strategies to Organize Your Life & Double Your Success*. I used the bones of my speech, combined them with stories and examples, and wrote my first book.

In the dozens of books that have followed, I have used what I consider a rather simple way to put together a nonfiction book. I suggest you use these same steps to write your own book (you guessed it) *like a boss.*

- What is your book's point of view?

- Decide the intention and purpose for the book.

- Answer the four key questions.

- Define your avatar, or ideal reader.

- Craft a detailed outline, focused on giving advice to one avatar, giving advice in a conversational style.

I'll break down my process for you, describing each step (and the thought process behind it). This will allow you to write your own nonfiction book as easily and effortlessly as possible. The book you'll be able to write will work on your behalf, providing key information to the reader, and perhaps will connect you with those you can personally help.

I could just tell you how to outline your book, but without some forethought, you will be left with a book that won't serve you at the highest level. So kindly allow me to walk you through a process that will result in a book you love, and one that impacts the world and perhaps your business in just the way you want.

Who Writes a Nonfiction Book?

The person who writes a nonfiction book is generally a professional who wants to increase their profile, establish their brand, and as a result, charge more for their products or services (or both). Another reason is because they've survived tough life circumstances and want to share their story and what they've learned in the hope of saving someone else from similar trouble.

Whatever your reason, you have probably been told, or know intuitively, you must write a book. I promise you that while it is work, it isn't as difficult or time-consuming as you might imagine. With the right preparation, you can feel as though you're sailing through the writing process.

Expert or Reporter?

Before you begin, there's one decision to make: from which viewpoint will you be writing? If you've been in business for more than five years, you have experience and information you share on a regular basis. You can organize it into a readable format, and turn it into a solid book. This means you'll be writing from the *expert's perspective*.

An *expert* writes most their book's content from stream-of-consciousness—i.e., they already possess the knowledge their book will contain. Writing their book is simply a matter of taking what they already know, organizing it, and getting it down on paper.

If you've been in business or in your current position five years or less, you would still benefit greatly from writing a book. You'll need to research the best content for your book, so you will write from the *reporter's perspective*, much like Napoleon Hill did in *Think and Grow Rich*.

A *reporter* may have a solid knowledge base, and will need to research and gather additional valuable information to convey to their readers. Of course, they will add their own perspective to the book. This type of book will take a bit longer to write. I'll describe more about that later in this chapter.

The Intention and Purpose of Your Book

Defining the intention and purpose of your book is a critical step. With some forethought, you can write an incredible book that works on your behalf for years to come, and provides multiple streams of income.

Unfortunately, I see this step skipped much of the time—which means there are lots of books written and published that languish in obscurity or simply disappoint their authors.

Not good.

Your intention for your book can be defined by answering this question: *In an ideal world, what will happen with the book?*

Pam Grout, author of *E-Squared*, wanted to sell millions of copies of her book and inspire those millions of readers. That was her intention, and she wrote it in sand on a beach. Intention set.

What do you want to happen with your book? Nonfiction books aren't usually turned into movies, but they can become *New York Times* bestsellers or *the book everybody is reading* (such as *The Miracle Morning* or *The One Thing*). You get to decide what you want to set as your intention for your book, and I highly suggest you do!

Next, you'll define your book's purpose. The purpose of the book is *to do* something—in other words, what do you want the book *to do* for the reader? Here are a few examples: help the reader understand why they need an estate plan, or why they need to start investing early, or how to lose weight with your approach to diet and exercise.

This step is especially important because it can have a variety of answers, and each one will change how you write. Here are a couple of examples of potential purposes.

1. The Business Builder. If you want to write the book to build your business, this is likely your answer. You may or may not write other books because your primary goal is NOT to write full-time, but to boost your existing brand or business. A book can be the best type of business card and can help boost your business in a dramatic way.

2. The Expert. If you are an expert in your field and you want to leverage your knowledge into a writing career, this is probably your answer. Honorée is a perfect example of this one, because she used her wealth of knowledge to expand into writing. This strategy typically involves writing full-time, and consistent writing is key. Keep that in mind when you are planning your content because you may outline several books in a series rather than one title.

3. The World Changer. If you have a specialized knowledge that you think will effect change—whether your target is a club or a country—writing a book is probably your answer. You may intend to write a few books or only one, or to build a career, but knowing your end game will change how you write.

4. The Memoir Writer. Whether you've lived a public life or a private one, your story is unique. The Memoir Writer usually wants to tell their own story, and if you fit into this category I applaud you. But keep in mind that one book can be a segue to others. And if you're going to write a book, do it right.

These are just four examples that you may fit into, but they do not constitute a complete list. You may fit into more than one, and that's perfectly fine. What's important is that you define your book's purpose, because doing so will set the foundation for what you want. As we said at the beginning, set your vision and make sure your book's purpose is aligned with that.

I've met authors who say they want to write full-time but they consistently write books that don't support that goal. If your actions do not align with your vision, your vision will go unrealized.

Like Ben and I have said, defining your purpose will alter how you write. Now that you have, let's get into the next step.

The Four Key Questions:

Your answers to the Four Key Questions will inform and influence the contents of the book in a strategic way. For the book to work on your behalf, you must have clean, clear answers to these questions:

1. **"What's in it for me?"** In other words, what do you want from your book, specifically? A stream, or multiple streams, of income? The flow of new clients? The ability to charge more for your products or services? A bigger brand presence? To set you apart from your competition?

2. **"What do I want the reader to do?"** For *You Must Write a Book*, I want every reader to write a book! And, I want them to have the confidence they can write it, and the technical knowledge to publish it.

3. **"What do I want them to avoid doing?"** Again, for *You Must Write a Book,* I want the reader to

avoid writing a book of poor quality. There is a lot of information encouraging people to quickly write and publish a book with little or no regard for quality or content. I know from experience the regret one can feel from publishing a book without thinking it through.

4. **"What do I want the 'right' reader to do?"** I want the right (or perfect-for-me) reader to hire me as their coach. This is not an overt message, but because I share my expertise, many people have decided they won't want to "figure it out" themselves and would rather have a guide (me) to help them. Many of your readers could use your book as the basis for hiring you or purchasing your products. Note: The book doesn't need to be an overt high-pressure sales pitch. To the contrary: The more information you share, the better the perception of your expertise by the reader.

Take a few minutes and answer the Four Key Questions. Next, you get to identify your ideal reader.

Are you having fun yet? I hope so! I love the process of crafting my book. I hope you do, too.

Who Is Your Avatar?

Once you've gained clarity about your perspective as an author and answered the Four Key Questions, you must identify the exact person your book's content would benefit. This is your avatar, also known as your ideal reader.

When I write each book in *The Prosperous Writer* book series, my avatar is a writer who:

- Has been writing for years

- Wants to make a living as a writer

- Is between 30-50 years of age

- Can be either male or female

- Has or has had a career, but not one they enjoy as much as writing

Honorée knows WAY more than I do when it comes to writing nonfiction, but this point is especially important. Making this list will be crucial when you begin your marketing efforts because you've just defined your target market. These attributes are what you'll use to help target your ideal readers on programs like Facebook. Doing it now gives you a head start and makes sure your book will hit its desired target.

The Business Book

If you're writing a business book, your ideal reader will most likely mirror your ideal client. A list of at least ten qualities and characteristics of your ideal client (and reader) will keep you focused as you determine your book's content. If you can get up to twenty-five qualities and characteristics on your list (or more), all the better.

Why is this list important? You can't, and don't, give the same advice to every customer or client. Similarly, it is impossible to include advice *for everyone* in your book.

You must pick a lane and stay in it—you must point most of your book's advice in one general direction. The best way to make sure you do that is to write to one person or one type of person. Your advice will be applicable to the lion's share of the people who read your book. And, again, if someone wants your professional advice for their specific situation, they can connect with you and ask!

The General Advice Book

If you're writing a general advice book, you still need to define your avatar. You shouldn't attempt to include advice for everyone (that would be one long book!). Pinpointing a specific type of person will still help you connect to those who fall outside of your identified avatar without you writing a prohibitively long book.

I started writing *Prosperity for Writers* because, while attending a writer's conference, I heard writer after writer bemoan the fact that while they were terrific writers, they didn't believe they could make a living as a writer. I know *for a fact* that making a living as a writer is an inside job (you must get your mind right!), and I was inspired to share my process for prospering as a writer. My avatar was one of the attendees: a woman, in her mid-30s, who was struggling financially because she didn't believe she could make a living as a writer.

While I didn't even entertain the idea of writing a series at first, the book really struck a nerve with readers and I was inspired to keep writing. Each subsequent book answers a specific question, all going back to how to prosper as a writer. Why do I mention this? Because your first book may not be your last, and perhaps could become a series.

In *You Must Write a Book*, I wrote to an actual person. Eric Negron is a former business coaching client, financial advisor, a friend, and someone I know for sure would benefit from having a book.

You can take the approach that you think will work best for you. Take some time and identify your avatar. Once that's finished, you're ready to begin your outline.

Your Book's Outline: The Topic, Table of Contents, and more...

As I start outlining a book, I imagine a conversation I've had with an avatar. Those who want to write a book always tend to ask the same questions. In my mind, I walk through our conversation from beginning to end, including the questions I get on a regular basis, and the answers I give. To me, this is the easiest and most effective way to determine what content should be included.

1. Choose your book's topic.

What is the topic you want to tackle in your book? Most likely, the topic you choose will be based on the multiple, similar conversations you've had with your clients, and the advice you've shared.

A business attorney may choose to write about the different types of companies to form based on the different tax advantages and protections provided. A speaker who focuses on leadership will write a book on leadership principles or how to become a better leader. A stylist could write about a capsule wardrobe, how to dress for one's body type, or what to wear for special occasions.

The topic of your book will logically lead to the identification of the subtopics you'll focus on in the book.

2. Create a Table of Contents

After brainstorming your book's topic and subtopics, organize them into their logical order. This becomes the beginning of your table of contents. If done correctly (you go into enough detail in your subtopics), you'll find you have a rather detailed table of contents with chapter titles and subheading titles. However, at first you might create a simple outline or a bulleted list—this is what happens with me. I identify my main topic and five to ten subtopics. I do a deeper outline later.

Whatever your method of choice, create something that looks like the structure of a book. You'll know, based on your expertise, what content will fill that structure as you create your manuscript.

As you sit down to write each day, you know exactly what to write. You'll see each topic, and write the content. The more detailed your outline, the faster and easier you will be able to write your book. In fact, you won't spend much time wondering what to write next—you'll see the next topic, think of the question you're answering, and then write as though you were speaking directly to your avatar. You'll use your outline, in the form of your table of contents, to write your book all the way to the conclusion.

Two key additions: your introduction and your conclusion. I write my introduction after I've completed the first draft, so I can allude to what is to come. The conclusion is a call-to-action meant to inspire my readers to take immediate action on what they've learned, and you may want to use that approach also.

3. Determine What Research You Need

You may be able write your book without much additional research because you are the expert on the topic. If, however, you're reporting on a topic, you'll require research and the time to conduct it. In either instance, you will discover a need to search for something—a URL, a quote, or the title of a book (which slow down progress just a bit). Preparation can help keep your fingers on the keyboard, typing, rather than perusing the Internet.

Once you have your detailed table of contents, identify the possible research you need and make note of it. When I see a quote that's useful as I'm scrolling through Facebook or Instagram, I take a screenshot to use later. I keep notes in my Bullet Journal to reference as I'm writing. And I keep a page at the end of my manuscript with different notes or ideas as they occur to me (just so I don't have to try to remember them, which I inevitably won't).

If you discover, as you're writing, that you need more research or interviews, keep writing. Write some text with a note and highlight it to refer to later. When it's time to go through your manuscript again, you'll see the highlighted parts and be able to address and knock them out in no time.

4. Create a To-Do List

Once you have your outline nailed down, go through it and determine if there's any research not related to writing you want to complete before you start writing. In my to-do list, I include the URLs I want to include, books I want to reference for passages or quotes, or even articles I might want to refer to. You also might want to conduct interviews.

5. Gather and Organize Your Materials

Before you begin writing, gather your research and materials and put them where they are accessible. As I mentioned, I use my Bullet Journal to compile notes and then place them all at the end of the actual manuscript document. I also use Dropbox to keep everything related to the project (manuscript, notes, URLs, and other resources) so I can always get what I need when I need it.

Have as much of what you need to write your book accessible before you start work on your manuscript. This will make your life easier, and the process of writing your book faster (and much less painful). You can use any combination of handwritten notes, file folders, computer folders, or cloud storage—whatever works best for you. Only you know what system will make your writing process a positive experience!

How Long Will It Take to Write?

Nonfiction books generally run between 25,000 and 75,000 words. My books usually run between 30,000 to 50,000 words. The amount of time it takes to write a book is determined by the target number of words divided by the daily word count. At two thousand words a day, I can crank out a 50,000-word book in twenty-five writing days. If your book requires research, it will take longer to write (or at least a bit more time to get organized). If you dictate your book, getting the main content out of your head and on paper might take much less time. I love utilizing Dragon Dictation to speak my content and watch the words magically appear on the screen. I suggest experimenting with the different ways to write until you find your groove and what works best for you.

Writing from your own expertise will take less time. Unless you're using anecdotes, quotes, or other people's stories, you might be able to sail through your manuscript in short order.

A quick way to determine how long (ballpark) it will take you to write your book is to do some word sprints. Word sprints are timed writing sessions. Set a timer and write for twenty or even thirty minutes, uninterrupted, as quickly as you can. Use your word count to estimate the amount of time your entire project will take.

Keep in mind that you will write better and faster (dare I say, *like a boss*) when you ruthlessly focus on the task at hand, in this case, *writing*. I remove all distractions for the sixty or ninety minutes I write every day, getting my time and the words in, and then move on with the rest of my day. Even when I have only a few minutes, I put in earbuds and listen to an inspiring playlist while I write. Ultimately, to become a professional, full-time writer you will need to bank a lot of words and potentially volumes of work. The only way to do it *is to do it.*

Predetermine Your Writing Schedule (and Commit to It)!

If you don't write when you don't have time for it, you won't write when you do have time for it.
—Katerina Stoykova-Klemer

You now know approximately how much time you will need to write your book. You next step is to find those hours in your calendar and block them off. I like to estimate the number of days I'll need to complete a project and then set an appointment on my calendar for each day (with a reminder that pops up ten minutes ahead of time).

My calendar is set for me to write from 6-7 a.m. during the school year, and from 6-7:30 a.m. during the summer and holiday breaks. Be sure to overestimate the amount of time it will take, and allow more hours than you think necessary for "unforeseen circumstances," such as sick days, missed days, vacations, holidays, friend and family interruptions (you get the gist).

My writing hours are sacred. Once the alarm goes off, I stop whatever else I'm doing and get ready to write. I set another alarm for when it's time to stop and write as much as I can, staying as focused as I can, until my writing session is over. I also keep track of my word count for each writing session. Some days I write just a few hundred words, some days a few thousand. Over time, the words rack up and I can see I am making real progress and it encourages me to keep going.

Here are a few tips to set you up to write like a boss:

- Find a quiet place where you won't be interrupted.

- Please, silence your cell phone (just like in the movie theater). Limited distractions equal maximum productivity.

- Get an accountability partner or writing buddy. Check in before you begin writing, and then share your word counts after.

- Your writing sessions are appointments you are making with yourself. They should be inviolate, just like any other professional appointment.

Keep track of your word count and make a commitment to write a minimum number of words each day (And don't forget, even 100 words a day counts!). Seeing your word count increase will help you stay focused and encourage you because you'll see real progress on each project every day. Keeping track of your word count may seem pointless, because you already know what you accomplished, but it will help you identify your average word count. Tracking it makes it possible to improve it, and that is essential to building a consistent writing habit.

With the right preparation, planning, and execution, you can *write like a boss*. In fact, owning your role as a professional writer is easier than you think. Use our suggestions as your guide, and feel free to adjust them to fit you, your personality, and how you work the best.

6

You Can Do It, So Do It

B en and I both agreed the last chapter of this book must have a strong send-off. Our goal was to give you the tools you need to feel unstoppable— like you could transform your writing production from aspirational to exceptional.

Are you feeling armed with what you need to be unstoppable? Perhaps there's a little bit more we can say to urge you forward.

Consider this: *No ultra-prolific writer started out that way!*

I wrote my first book in a weekend because I was dictating a speech into a book (then I was *so over it* I didn't look at it again for months). My second book took months and months and months, mostly because I spent an awful lot of time thinking I needed to write but not writing. When I did finally get to the point where I would sit down to write, I would stare at a blinking cursor and have no idea what to do. Should I write the first chapter, or revisit the outline, or call someone and interview them? It was frustrating and did nothing for my self-esteem, that's for sure! I found it much more fun to discuss my upcoming book than to write it.

It wasn't until I was several books into my career that I began to systematize my writing process for maximum productivity and happiness.

Keep a vision in mind of who you want to become. Hold tightly to the mental picture you have of yourself as a prolific, masterful, and successful writer. Then, every day, move a little closer in reality to what you hold in mind.

We've talked about doubt and courage and given you the tools, but at the end of the day, only you can write your book. In today's market, every book has a readership, which means that there are readers waiting for what you have yet to write. It may seem daunting when you see other authors that seem so successful, but in reality they stood in your shoes just a few years ago. More than likely, they are using the very tools we've outlined for you in this book. They too will face doubt and discouragement, and the only edge they have is that they've faced it before.

Despite following their footsteps, you are forging your own path. We have seen countless writers rise and fall, and the biggest difference is not the market, the genre, or the style. It's the writer's drive. Find yours and be relentless in pursuit of your vision!

This Is Your Journey, and Yours Alone

In addition, there's one other distinction I want to make sure you know: you're not in competition with any other writer on this planet. In fact, you're not in competition at all. Your best bet is to become the best writer you can possibly be, to find out what you're made of—what you're truly capable of! It doesn't matter that some writers publish a book every two weeks, or write one book and get a movie deal. That's their journey. This is yours!

Comparing yourself to others may only serve to cause you paralysis. I've seen "comparisonitis" become the basis of jealousy, unhealthy competition, and even territorial bridge burning (and that was just in my first year of author networking!).

If anything, watching other writers produce and succeed should serve as a shining light guiding you to what is possible *for you*. If someone else can write five thousand words in a day, so can you. If a writer can sell his self-published book to Hollywood and have a blockbuster movie, there's no reason why you can't!

I LOVE what Honorée said here. As a writer, your greatest adversary is you—but so is your greatest ally. The book market is bigger than you can imagine and there is plenty of room for everyone. Quality content tends to rise, but more importantly, writing your passion means you connect with people who share the same passion. When you write with emotion they will feel it, whether it's fiction or nonfiction.

At its core, writing is a medium to convey information and evoke emotion. Few write solely for their own benefit, and most are trying to connect with others. Whomever you are trying to connect with, keep them in mind as you write because they are the other side of the conversation. They will hear you. They will become your fans. They will tell their friends and your words will spread. You want to know how to achieve an impossible dream? Make your words contagious.

Set your sights high, keep taking consistent steps in the directions of your dreams, and eventually you will arrive at your destination. I like to joke that I'm a thirty-year overnight success—and it's true! I've been working day in and day out since (literally) 1987. "All of a sudden" here I am!

Never give up, keep building your bookshelf and your faith in yourself, and you will get where you're going sooner than later.

You might get a lightning strike and find your goldmine sooner rather than later. (It hasn't happened to me yet!) If this happens, mazel tov and great for you! But if, like me, it takes a really long time, that's okay too. You're a writer and that's so cool! Enjoy each word you write, cherish every writing session. I know for a fact there are so many people who would push their grandmother down a flight of stairs to be able to write for a living (just kidding, but are you really reading this?).

But, You're Not Alone!

Remember, you may have to write alone, but you can build a community of other writers. As one of my fellow writers said to me this past week, *I'm so glad we're talking! There are very few people who truly understand what I'm talking about.* Indeed, having writer friends for the purposes of collaboration, accountability, ideas, and, of course, some good-old fashioned fun is the best!

I have monthly author dinners with my Austin author friends, regular Skype chats with friends who live far away, and a daily phone chat with my author buddy Brian Meeks.

Doing writing sprints at the same time as other writer friends is fun, spirited, and productive. You can organize in-person write-ins and virtual productivity sessions. You can find other like-minded folks to collaborate with on fun projects, fiction or nonfiction.

The king of all things fiction collaboration is Michael Anderle, who, with his co-authors, manages to pump out several books a month.

Honorée is so right here. The author community is huge, and tapping into it is awesome. I too have dinners with authors whenever the occasion permits. Writing can be a solitary occupation and meeting with authors in person is both inspiring and fun. You get to pool ideas and share heartaches, and just laugh at shared experiences. You can find authors EVERYWHERE, so find a group to join and have a blast.

Keep in mind that different groups have different purposes. Some writer's groups focus on the writing, and share their work in an effort to improve. I attended one for a year before I published my first book, and it proved to be an enormous help. Other groups are speaker oriented and bring in individuals to help authors learn from authors or professionals in a variety of fields. These too can be a great benefit. Keep in mind you can always start your own. When I first published I couldn't find a group that talked about indie publishing so I started my own on a site, Meetup.com. I kept it going for a year and am still friends with many people I met at that group.

At the current moment I focus more on writing sprints, frequently with a good friend of mine, Chanda Hahn. We both like to write clean fiction, so we meet on Skype and sprint write for 45 minutes and then break for 15. When I do these sprints, I can usually knock out 1,400–1,500 words in an hour! Doing just a couple can fill my entire word count for the day. Don't let writing be a solitary job. Reach out and find a tribe, and you will be stunned by the support you find. They won't just be writer friends, they will be true friends for life.

It's up to you to seek out new connections and develop them into friendships. Here are a few ways to find amazing writer friends:

- **Writing Conferences.** There are so many fantastic conferences! My first was the *Colonists Summit*, which was the precursor to the *Smarter Artist Summit*, held annually by the co-hosts of the *Self-Publishing Podcast*, Sean Platt, Johnny B. Truant, and David Wright. In fact, I met two of my best writer friends there, Brian D. Meeks and, of course, Ben Hale!

This list is so big! You've got UTOPiAcon in Nashville, Penned Con (a personal favorite) in St. Louis, the Florida Writer's Association State Conference in Orlando, the Smarter Artist Summit in Austin Texas, Novelist, Inc. (NINC, for published authors), Dragon Con, Ozark Book Fest, RT (Romantic Times Convention), and so many more. Some of these conferences are tailored to writers and readers, allowing you to sell books as well as connect with other writers. Keep in mind that the greatest value of these events is the connections you make. Within a few years these specific events might be gone, but the writers don't go away. You'll find them traveling and uniting and new events. Find them. Join them. Learn. And have a blast!

Pro Tip: When you get done with an event, make a list of all the people you met. Then write any ideas you received from them in a column next to it. Then finish by putting the value of the ideas in a third column and add it up for the estimated value of the event. Remember when I described this technique? This is an example in action.

I went to an event once where the estimated value was $123,600!! If you doubt that number, consider what I learned at an event a year and a half ago. My audio producer said that the choice in narrator is a $100,000 decision. I sold my audio rights to them four years ago and to date my audio books have earned over $100,000. In a moment I'll talk about the value of a word count, and it will blow your mind!

- **Online.** There are countless groups for writers on Facebook, including the one I host, *The Prosperous Writer Mastermind.* Michael Anderle started the 20Booksto50K group, and it has over ten thousand members as of this writing. Brian D. Meeks has Mastering Amazon Ads. No matter what type of writing you do, you'll find a group that will make you feel welcome and at home.

- **Writer's Groups.** Meetup.com is a great place to find writing groups in your area. In fact, you can find groups on this site for just about anything.

Here are a few online groups I would highly recommend joining. First would be Indie Writer's Unite. This is also a Facebook group that has authors ranging from just starting out to incredibly experienced. Post a question there and you can usually get quick answers. Keep in mind that it's a zero-promotion site, so if you have a new release, don't post it in the group.

Second is another Facebook group called Club Indie. This group also forbids promotion, and they are a little more selective in who they accept, but it's a great collection of authors.

Third, as Honorée suggested, Meetup.com. This website allows you to search for and join a group of like-minded individuals, and includes anything from snowboarders to chess aficionados, and yes, it has writers. Go to the site and see if a group is in the area. There are probably more than you might think!

- **Reach out!** I've made quite a few friends by reaching out to authors and writers I admire. If I can, I'll get an introduction. If not, I'll send an email or connect with them via Facebook, Twitter, Instagram, or even LinkedIn.

- **Ask,** *Who should I know?* This is a question to ask yourself and others who know you well. I was introduced to Charlie Hoehn by a mutual friend, and what a great person he is! We'll talk about this more in both *Publishing Like a Boss* and *Marketing Like a Boss*, because intentional connections and friendships are key to any writer's success.

Finding other writers will serve to make you feel more normal and accepted by others. Even when your other friends and family don't understand your compulsion to write, or they dismiss your career choice as "less than legit" or a "recipe for disaster," your writer friends will be there to encourage, inspire, and help you in countless ways.

You Can Do It, So Do It

The world is waiting for your words! There is someone who is ready to devour the story you have been meaning to tell, to feel as though your characters are long-lost friends they can only unite with in the pages of your stories.

There are countless individuals who could benefit from the lessons you've learned as a professional, take inspired action from your advice, or avoid pain and suffering because you took the time to memorialize your knowledge.

If, on the off chance, you hold a belief that "the book you write has already been written," *au contraire, mon ami!* You are the only person who can write what you must write. No other soul has your perspective, experience, sense of humor, or awesomeness.

We think it's time you closed the pages of this book, and started writing your own.

We're looking forward to seeing what you write!

Honorée is right, and we believe in you. We may not know you personally, but we've met thousands of authors that are just starting their journey. You and they might share the same questions, and hopefully this book has given you some answers. I told you before that I'd share the value of a word count—a great point to end on. Consider for a moment the impact of increasing your average word count by 1,000 words a day. That's usually an hour or two, depending on the author. Doing that five days a week for fifty weeks a year (you won't work every week—you're not a machine!) will add up to 250,000 words. Keep doing it for ten years, taking your total word count to 2.5 million words.

Keep in mind this is on top of what you are already doing. If your average book is 80,000 words, in ten years you will have written an additional thirty-one books! If you estimate that your book will earn $10,000—which isn't a high number at all—that means that increasing your word count is a **$300,000 idea**!

This example is just the beginning. If you gradually increase your word count to 3,000 words a day, which is what I'm doing right now, the value of this one idea reaches **$1,000,000**!

We've given you all the tools, and this example proves it. Now gather your courage and get ready, because your career is about to start. And just like Honorée said, never think that your story has already been written. Every story may have been told, **but your voice has yet to be heard**. Your readers await your story. Be Relentless. Be Undaunted.

Be a Writer.

QUICK FAVOR

We're wondering, did you enjoy this book?

First of all, thank you for reading our book! May we ask a quick favor?

Will you take a moment to leave an honest review for this book? Reviews are the BEST way to help others purchase the book.

You can go to the link below and write your thoughts. We appreciate you!

HonoreeCorder.com/WriteLABReview

WHO IS HONORÉE?

Honorée Corder is the author of dozens of books, including the *Like a Boss* book series, *You Must Write a Book, I Must Write My Book, The Prosperous Writer Book Series, Vision to Reality, Business Dating, The Successful Single Mom* book series, *If Divorce is a Game, These are the Rules*, and *The Divorced Phoenix*.

She is also Hal Elrod's business partner in *The Miracle Morning* book series. Honorée coaches business professionals, writers, and aspiring nonfiction authors who want to publish their books to bestseller status, create a platform, and develop multiple streams of income. She also does all sorts of other magical things, and her badassery is legendary. You can find out more at HonoréeCorder.com.

Honorée Enterprises, Inc.
Honorée@HonoréeCorder.com
http://www.HonoréeCorder.com
Twitter: @Honorée
& @Singlemombooks
Facebook: http://www.facebook.com/Honorée

WHO IS BEN?

Ben Hale is the best-selling author of the Chronicles of Lumineia. Originally from Utah, Ben grew up with a passion for learning. Drawn particularly to reading, he was caught reading by flashlight under the covers at a young age. While still young, he practiced various sports, became an Eagle Scout, and taught himself to play the piano. This thirst for knowledge gained him excellent grades and helped him graduate college with honors, as well as become fluent in three languages after doing volunteer work in Brazil. After school, he started and ran several successful businesses that gave him time to work on his numerous writing projects.

Ben launched his first book in 2012, and six months later he sold his business and began writing full-time. Since then he has published 17 titles across five series within the fantasy world of Lumineia. To date his series has sold 200,000 copies and continues to garner praise from readers. His greatest support comes from his wonderful wife and six beautiful children. Currently he resides in Missouri while working on his Masters in Professional Writing.

To contact Ben, discover more about Lumineia, or find out about upcoming sequels, check out his website at Lumineia.com. You can also follow him on twitter @BenHale8 or Facebook.

www.ingramcontent.com/pod-product-compliance
Lightning Source LLC
Chambersburg PA
CBHW071134280326
41935CB00010B/1222